W9-CCW-153

**to the
end
of the
earth**

MISSION CONCEPT IN PRINCIPLE AND PRACTICE

to the
end
of the
earth

BY ROLF A. SYRDAL

Augsburg Publishing House
Minneapolis, Minnesota

27969

TO THE END OF THE EARTH

MANUFACTURED IN THE UNITED STATES OF AMERICA

DEDICATED

To my wife

INTRODUCTION

The theological bases for the motives and methods of world mission have not been given the emphasis they deserve. Popular presentation of the story of mission has usually been limited to missions in action. Stories of the lives and deeds of Christian missionaries have often been a source of inspiration. Individual missionaries of exceptional gifts and attainments have been singled out and have been portrayed as personalities of epic stature. On the other hand, the average missionary has often been pictured as a well-meaning, dedicated man spending his life fighting fevers in inhospitable climates and trying, with only minimal success, to elevate the people of an underdeveloped country. His contribution to the total program and impact of mission may be as valuable as that of the more rare "hero."

The pioneer missionary had to serve as explorer, hunter, teacher, builder, pastor, healer, advisor, and bishop as he established and administered schools, organized congregations, trained preachers, and laid foundations for indigenous churches. His was a herculean task that demanded more than he had to give. The challenge raised him in stature and made him realize his dependence on the Holy Spirit to accomplish what he in his own power never could. Today the task remains staggering, but it is shared by men of different talents and training, and by leaders and pastors of the indigenous churches.

The story of world mission is more than the biography of missionaries. It is more than a group of individuals knit together for the purpose of carrying out a noble program. Mission is the purposeful act of God who desires "all men to be saved and come to the knowledge of the truth" (1 Tim. 2:4). It is God who initiated mission, and it is he who calls and empowers the church and individuals within the church to carry out the work.

Mission is the function of the church, which is "the body of Christ on earth." The program of the church is divine. The nature of the church, and its effectiveness in carrying out the will of God, are influenced by its members. They, in turn, are influenced by various movements and attitudes in the world which have repercussions in the church and affect its program. During periods of rationalism, skepticism has dampened missionary zeal within the church. During the romantic period, characterized by spreading colonialism and daring exploits to conquer the unknown, mission leaders were optimistic and adopted the slogan "the evangelization of the world in this generation." During our present period of international tension and insecurity, of literary realism, impressionistic art, and philosophical nihilism, man's focus has been drawn to himself, and his attitude is one of frustrated cynicism. The result is an existentialism that goes no farther than man's experience for the moment. God, objective spiritual realities, and a divine goal are eliminated. To the extent that this spirit influences the people within the church, missions will be regarded as a vague, unrealistic dream of the past.

The mission program must be seen in light of its eternal pattern. In the early twentieth century, following a period of rationalism in the church, Hendrik Kraemer sought to bring mission back to the center of Christian thinking and action by facing the consequences of what he calls "biblical realism." This realism is the recognition that man is depraved and lost; that he was created for fellowship with God; and that God therefore seeks to save him and enable him to live in the regenerate state as the child of God. This is accomplished in Jesus Christ. The natural conclusion that must be drawn from our Christian faith, in every age and under every type of human influence, is the same.

> One demand universally emerges from the situation everywhere, that is, back to the recapturing of the vision of what God in

Christ meant the Christian Community to be—a fellowship of
believers, rooted in God and His divine redemptive order, and
therefore committed to the service and the salvation of the
world; going to the bottom in its criticism of and opposition
to the evil of the world, but at the same time going to the bottom
in its identification with the sufferings and needs of the world.[1]

The purpose of this study of world mission is to determine the
nature of mission as found in the Bible and to trace the progress of
mission through various periods of history. It is hoped that the
nature, objectives, methods, and procedures of missions may be
more fully understood in light of failures and successes, and that
mission in our day may take on a new perspective in light of God's
plan for the world.

CONTENTS

Introduction

CHAPTER ONE

MISSION MOTIVATION AND PURPOSE

We, as a church, have inherited missions as a responsibility, as one of the activities of the organized church to which we belong. Personal, vital interest in the program is often lacking. It is an activity in which many members are only indirectly involved.

Altogether too common is the attitude that missions are a necessary and commendable project that someone else should develop and support. Stimulation for the work, following a special presentation by a returned missionary, is often short-lived. Within the church there are always the few who have the vision, and continue to do what they can for the cause. Others may regard it as a less important, peripheral activity of the church. Still others may recognize the need for missions, but they feel that by establishing a division of the church for the purpose of carrying out the program, the individual member is absolved from direct responsibility.

A similar attitude has developed toward the missionary. It cannot be said of the average church that each member is a missionary consciously and purposefully. The fact that he is a missionary-of-sorts, whether he wills it or not, is frightening. The sincere missionary is labeled. He is a member often looked at with some skeptical admiration as noble "but a little bit different."

In contrast, during the apostolic period, mission was certainly taken for granted. Very little time was spent in trying to establish the correct philosophical or theological approach to mission. It was simply accepted that proclaiming the Gospel was the central

1

purpose of the church and the responsibility of each Christian. It was not long before the study of missions began, basically as a reply to opposition from without the church. As the church grew and became rooted in many lands of varied traditions, and as its organization developed, mission work became more specialized. The studies dealt with the Bible and its message and with the needs of the people of the world, reflecting from both angles the responsibility of the church. This dual approach remains the foundation for the continued study of missions, but there are many divisions and specific questions confronted as each age seeks answers for its own problems. The study of missions by the church is nothing new. For the first few generations it was not necessary to justify missions. Most of what was written was aimed to stimulate greater zeal on the part of many for the work, rather than to develop a complete theology of mission. This continued to be true till the day of rationalism in comparatively recent times.

Through the centuries, various motives have inspired Christians to mission activity[1]:

1. **Philanthropic Motive.** This motive has been consistently apparent in the history of missions—especially in the period of European colonial expansion. The dominant, optimistic spirit of the West came into contact with people living in a state that was considered pitiful. Early explorers and missionaries described these conditions, and kindled both Christian and humanitarian sympathy which led to action. There is no way of measuring the lasting material benefits brought to many countries through the witness and work of missions. Suttee and the evils of child brides have been abolished; cannibalism and slavery have disappeared. Medical missions have improved the health of people. Education, introduced by the missionary in most of the so-called "mission areas," has raised the standard of living among the masses. No doubt an element of the philanthropic motive will continue, and *should* continue, as long as hearts beat in human love toward fellowmen. But this spirit has spread beyond the church. Today governments officially adopt aid-to-underdeveloped-nations programs of staggering size. Movements such as the "Peace Corps" of the United States, "Bread for the World" of Germany, and similar programs in England and the Scandinavian countries have been similarly motivated.

Theologically, this philanthropic motivation for missions is a natural result and manifestation of the love of God in the believer's heart. It has not been an end in itself. Changes in some countries of the world have made philanthropy less necessary. Japan with the highest literacy rate in the world and with its mastery in technology is a glowing example. In the new nations developing in Africa and Asia, rapid progress is expected in educational and economic fields so that the term "underdeveloped" may no longer be a fit description of them, though that situation will not be changed overnight. Meanwhile, the idea of philanthropy as the primary motive for missions is weakened. This may result in less support for missions from those who can see no other legitimate motive. On the other hand, there will be more freedom to emphasize the greater objectives of missions.

2. **Eschatological Motive.** This motive originally was associated with the term "pity the perishing heathen." Emphasis was put on the need to save as many as possible from hell or, in other words, simply to prepare people for the life hereafter. Some sought to hasten the coming of the day of the Lord's return, either as a millennial reign in present history or as a final judgment upon the earth. Early Americans interested in missions were stimulated by this motive, as shown in the writing of students promoting missionary work and in reports from the missionaries. The eschatological aspect was also present among these early Americans in their expectation of Christ's imminent return. Cotton Mather wrote directly to Ziegenbalg and Plutschau in India in 1717 as follows:

> It is most certain that God's prophecy has yet to be fulfilled: "I will pour out my Spirit upon all flesh." It is also probable that the pouring out of the Holy Spirit by which the Christian Church was founded is to be viewed merely as a matter of some drops, whereas at the end of the age, when the fulfilment of this prophecy will come, there will be a much more abundant rain. . . . I do not know whether the time will be soon at hand which is appointed by God for the pouring out of the Holy Spirit and whether the kingdom of God will be revealed soon. I believe, however, that it is at hand.[2]

During periods of rationalism this motive was scorned. In our day it has been revived, but with a new connotation. Salvation is not only other-worldly and for the hereafter. The eternal fellowship with God is to begin here and bear its fruits now. The consciousness that we are living "between the times" of Christ's first and second coming—between the establishment and the fulfillment of his Kingdom—has given an eschatological finality to the message of salvation and life with God in "the Now," and the assurance of the coming fulfillment. It complements the humanitarian view that works merely for the betterment of conditions in this world and does not limit the kingdom to the other-worldly future. Correctly understood, the eschatological motive has taken on new emphasis and importance in the theology of missions in our day.

3. **Theological Motive.** Peter's message on the Day of Pentecost ended with the statement: "Repent and be baptized every one of you in the name of Jesus Christ for the forgiveness of your sins; and you shall receive the gift of the Holy Spirit" (Acts 2:38). This statement presents a theological aim. To Jews and followers of other religions the purpose was the same. Let God, in Christ, be known to men that they may receive forgiveness of sins and live in his fellowship. Jesus is the Christ!

During one period of mission history, religions were compared with other religions and these, in turn, were compared with Christianity. Ethically minded men have found elements of high moral standards in many writings of other religions. Mystics have discovered elements in other religions that have gripped men to degrees of self-denial rarely seen in the average Christian community. Christianity has come to be considered by some merely as one of many religions. We have, however, learned to differentiate between religion and Christianity—between man's search for the divine or super-human and the faith which is given from God to man. God, in his love, has revealed himself, and man may accept this revelation. It is not man's religion but God's act that justifies. Christianity (as religion) is not to be compared with other religions, nor with paganism. There is no relevance in theological comparisons. Man is to be brought face to face with God in his mercy. Salvation in Christ is the *sui generis* message of the missionary which is needed by all men, whether they are renegade Christians or adherents of one of the world religions. God reveals "the Way." Men need to be in this Way both for this life and for eternal salvation.

This theological motive of mission is as pertinent in our enlightened age as in the more primitive period of history when God first revealed himself in the Christ who is the Way. The Christian does not join others in a common quest for God and for man's true relationship to God, for he already knows God and the way of life. But he does not approach the non-Christian with pride or a sense of superiority. He recognizes that he, like all men, is unable to accomplish his own salvation. He did not find God, but God found him. Redemption is God's free gift to all mankind. This is the message the Christian is impelled to tell others.

4. **Loyalty Motive.** This motive is described in the following words:

> Personal devotion to Christ is the impelling power, when to those who have heard His call to Salvation, *Come*, he utters His further call to service, *Go*.[3]

It can be illustrated from Isaiah. "And I heard the voice of the Lord saying 'Whom shall I send, and who will go for us?" Then I said, 'Here am I! Send me' (Is. 6:8). This spirit was manifested by other prophets and by the apostles. It has been an important factor in the decision of many men and women who became missionaries down through the ages. It was frequently mentioned in the early years of the student movement that gave rise to the mission work of the Protestant groups in America. Following the famous haystack prayer meeting of students in 1808, students at Williams and Andover Colleges formed a society to stir the church to its mission responsibility. The founders of this group presented their burden to the General Association of Congregational Ministers of Massachusetts, stating:

> that their minds have been long impressed with the duty and importance of personally attempting a mission to the heathen . . . and that, after examining all the information which they can obtain they consider themselves as devoted to this work for life, whenever God in His providence shall open the way.[4]

Loyalty to God ranks high as a directive for his people to carry on mission work. Standing alone, it might emphasize only the sovereignty of God, and therefore be legalistic. But it never stands alone. It is based on a vital, living relationship between God and man. It implies a change in man's nature that gives ready response both to God and to the needs of mankind. The love of God constrains him. "The Lord God has spoken; who can but prophesy?" (Amos 3:8).

5. Fraternal Motive.

> God deals not only with individuals as individuals, but with nations as nations, and with churches as churches, and for all alike the path of obedience is the only path of blessing.[5]

The fraternal motive results from the concept of the oneness of the world and the responsibility of the one part toward the others. "All under heaven are brothers." In the world—and often in the church—national and ethnic divisions and differences become walls of separation. In recognition of God's universal love for all men and all nations, these differences, for the Christian, should rather be bridges of contact. A pervading thought in the Old Testament is that God is God of the nations, not only of Judah. Isaiah spoke of Israel as the servant of the nations. The New Testament demonstrates throughout that God's love is universal and that we *are* our brothers' keepers. Jesus declared, "The Son of man came not to be ministered to, but to minister," and admonished his disciples, "give and it will be given to you . . . . "

6. **Filial Motive.** "Filial piety," a term used to describe the relationship of son to father, is especially strong in some Eastern countries where it takes on special meaning. It not only demands respect and obedience of son to father but includes respect and piety toward ancestors as far back as they can be traced. There is a recognition by the son of his membership in *the family*. There is no break between the generations. As a part of this family, he takes on its nature, its essence, and becomes a very part of it in its continuation.

The individual and the corporate body of Christians manifest the love of God, which is far above natural or human love. *Philia* is the Greek word for human love—a horizontal love, from man to man. It belongs to nature, and at its noblest is still not lifted above the natural. To express God's love, the word *agape* is used in the Bible. *Agape* is divine love—vertical, from God to man, higher than natural human love. The love of God is an attribute of God that is extended by him to the Christian. The church is to manifest the transformed nature of man. Mission becomes, not an imposed task or program, but the natural outflow of a redeemed nature that has within it the same love nature that Christ has. The summary of the life, death, and resurrection of Christ is found in Paul's words:

> Have this mind among yourselves, which you have in Christ Jesus, . . . that at the name of Jesus every knee should bow, in heaven and on earth and under the earth, and every tongue confess that Jesus Christ is Lord, to the glory of God the Father (Phil. 2:5, 10-11).

We are not only loyal to a command or enraptured by an ideal. We are "members of the household of God"; and its spirit, interests, and aims are therefore also ours. Conformity to the will of God is not an extra thing that constrains the Christian, but a natural expression of his new relationship to God. Mission is not a laudable duty of the pious but an inner *must* that witnesses in spontaneous love *(agape)* to all men.

> For if I preach the gospel, that gives me no ground for boasting. For necessity is laid upon me. Woe to me if I do not preach the gospel! (1 Cor. 9:16).

Many attempts have been made to define the term "mission." It is derived from the Latin *missio,* "a sending." A missionary is "one who is sent." This implies that there is also one who sends. By extension of this term, the church or mission society which has assumed the responsibility for missions is today called "the sending agency." It seeks out and calls men and women to be sent and continues support till the task of Christian witness is consummated in the response of faith. The Book of Acts tells of the departure of Paul and Barnabas on their first missionary journey:

> Now in the church at Antioch there were prophets and teachers, Barnabas, Symeon who was called Niger, Lucius of Cyrene, Manaen a member of the court of Herod the tetrarch, and Saul. While they were worshiping the Lord and fasting, the Holy Spirit said, "Set apart for me Barnabas and Saul for the work to which I have called them." Then after fasting and praying they laid their hands on them and sent them off. So, being sent out by the Holy Spirit, they went . . . (Acts 13:1-4a).

The procedure was direct and plain. The church, sensing its missionary nature, under God's guidance called men to be sent. The record reads, "they . . . sent them off," and "being sent out by the Holy Spirit." Both the church and those who were sent recognized that they acted under the directive force of the Holy Spirit. Both were under compulsion to witness—the one, as the instrument of God, to *send;* the other, as the agent of God, to *go.* Since that time, this pattern for the establishment of missions has been followed by churches and mission societies.

Mission is too broad and involved to be squeezed into a definition that deals mainly with the organizational aspect of the movement. Mission began at the beginning of time with God. The apostles and other believers in Christ began their work under the power of the Holy Spirit at Pentecost after the pattern of Christ's work and under his command.

The recognition that mission is inherent in the Gospel of Christ is given more vital recognition in recent years than in the preceding decades of mission theology. When the Gospel is mentioned it is taken for granted that it must involve mission. The individual Christian and the Church are therefore equally involved in giving adequate expression to the nature of the Gospel.

Kraemer describes missions in connection with the church on earth, the Body of Christ:

> The prophets and Paul are all under a "must" of the living God. So is the Church, and her obedience to it entails behaving as one who is sent as a missionary. It is this missionary vocation of the Church which leads her constantly into the position to give a reasonable account of her stupendous and seemingly bigoted claim that there is no salvation in any other than in Christ. This reasonable account is needed, not for the sake of missions, but for the sake of the world, in order that this offensive exclusiveness may be understood in its real intent.[6]

Bavinck speaks of the mission of the church in its relationship to the course of history:

> The science of missions is . . . occupied with two states of affairs, the first of which is the divine calling and ordaining of the church and the second is the actual realization of its calling in the course of history.[7]

Berdyaev speaks of mission as the divine energy within the heart of man to share the blessing of Christ which he himself has received:

> Creativeness has two different aspects and we describe it differently according to whether we dwell upon the one or the other. It has an inner and an outer aspect. There is the primary creative act in which man stands, as it were, face to face with God, and there is the secondary creative act in which he faces other men and the world. . . . The truly moral motive is not fear of punishment and of hell, but of selfless disinterested love of God and of the divine in life, of truth and perfection and all positive values.[8]

These definitions illustrate to some degree the intimate relationship of mission to the church and to the individual Christian. This relationship has been only vaguely realized by the average member of the church. A prevalent view of the church is that it is an organization in which a person may "take out membership." A member participates only in that which might be of special interest to him. Groups of individuals outside the organized church sometimes form societies for carrying out missionary activity, giving the impression that such work is for the few and is not the task of the total church.

The church is the Body of Christ on earth, composed of individuals who have been redeemed by Christ and live in him. When we speak of the church, we refer to the total church. Theological differences and historical events have divided the church into denominations, but "the church" includes all individuals who are Christ's. In our time there has been a reemphasis on the church as the agency of God, committed to his program of salvation. The importance of mission for the church has been stated by Emil Brunner, "The Church exists by mission, just as a fire exists by burning."[9] To this, a reader added, "Without flame, no fire; without mission, no church!"[10] Dr. Edwin Lewis, a professor of systematic theology, writes:

> The Church as a witness is the Church in one of its most fundamental aspects. It is new creation of the Creator of the world. . . . The origin of the world and the origin of the Church are at one and the same ultimate point, and they look to one and the same ultimate purpose of God. A primal creative act

brought the world into being. A second primal act brought the Church into being, for the Church is inexplicable apart from Christ, and Christ is inexplicable apart from God. . . . Briefly, then, the Church is a fact because the incarnation of the Word is a fact, and its primary task is to be witness to the power which created it.[11]

On the other hand, we recognize that the church is in the world and its members are human. This human element, seen within the church, is likewise seen in mission. It is the human rather than the divine aspect in missions that is most evident to the casual observer. The contrasts of success and failure, power and weakness, wisdom and mistakes in policy and practice, are all visible. In the age of romanticism and optimism, the successes of mission were most evident. The contrast between the West and the East, in the age of exploration and expansion, was possibly less noticeable than the spiritual contrast between the Christian faith and primitive paganism. The results of the impact of Christianity upon these people were dramatic.

In our day of realism and pessimism, international restiveness, insecurity and changing patterns, there are new obstacles for missions. This age produces pessimistic cynics who are critical of the existing order of society and of the church with its activities. Terms such as colonialism, white supremacy, and paternalism have been heard in reference to missions in new dimensions that sometimes blind the viewer to that which is underneath, that which is enduring, that which is of God.

Missionaries have been their own severest critics. Conscious of mistakes that have been made, they have been alert to watch for aspects of their work that might weaken the final results. Even missionaries have, on occasion, been unjust in the undue severity of judgment on methods and practices of earlier days. Early missions demanded men and women of strong character, unafraid to take leadership and dauntless in their defense of the small minority groups of Christians who became the nuclei of the present churches in mission lands. Some of these strong leaders, who accomplished more than many of the present-day missionaries with all their advanced knowledge of the theory of mission, lived beyond the pioneering period into a new age. Some did not change methods to meet the new conditions. It is possible that today's younger missionaries and churchmen will, in time, have the same criticism leveled at them.

The present always sits in judgment on the past, but criticism, to be just, must always be made in the perspective of history. It must never be a blanket condemnation or justification of the total. As only a small segment of an iceberg can be seen above the water, so, in the work of missions, there is a deep solid movement underneath, unaffected by blame or praise, as the purposeful work of God. We should observe what is above the surface, but also study the depths to see the reality, the mass, the main body of mission.

World mission has always faced psychological, sociological, physical and moral barriers. It has often had the support of only the minority within the churches and lacked even the tacit approval of the church's leaders. At the time when mission work was blossoming forth under the pietists of Francke,

> The Divinity Faculty of Wittenberg denounced missionary advocates as false prophets. In 1722 the hymnologist Neumeister of Hamburg closed his Ascensiontide sermon by giving out the hymn: " 'Go out into the world' the Lord of old did say; But now: Where God has placed thee, There He would have you stay!"[12]

In spite of the difficulties and in spite of the frailties of men who have been in the forefront of mission work, there are today vital indigenous churches in most lands where the Gospel was unknown 150 years ago. But, though there has been rapid progress in some areas, the growth of the church has not kept pace with the population increase in the world. The world is becoming proportionately more pagan year by year, in spite of Christian efforts at evangelism. In all of the major so-called mission areas of the world the church remains a minority group. In some places it is less than one percent of the population, struggling against tradition and family customs, but usually maintaining its indigenous and courageous nature.

> The great masses of Asia remain apparently impervious to the appeal of the Gospel. The Churches are, to outward seeming, very much like Western cultural colonies precariously situated on the edge of the old societies, tolerated chiefly because they show no signs of threatening the old faiths. They are heavily dependent, both spiritually and financially, on continuing sup-

port from the West. They are divided along the lines of the historic cultural divisions of Western Europe and, in spite of some movements towards unity, they show very little sign of becoming strong united and uniting bodies within the cultural life of their nations. They show little power of spontaneous growth and depend rather upon a continual flow of resources from outside to keep them where they are. Though eyes of faith may see them as the first-fruits of the people of Asia and Africa, eyes not so lighted will be inclined to write them off as the ineffectual remnants of the era of Western dominance—comparable to the little communities of Eastern Christians that survived the end of the first great missionary period of Christianity and the rise of the power of Islam.[13]

The picture of present-day missions presents a real challenge. With the resurgence of non-Christian religions appearing as nationalistic banners in some areas of the world, with the encroachment of atheistic communism, and with the solidification and intensification of Muslim aggression, there is need for a restudy of both the theology and the methodology of missions.

CHAPTER TWO

THE OLD TESTAMENT
AND MISSION

If the cause of world mission were a human enterprise it would not have lasted until today. It takes more than humanitarianism, idealism, and fanatical zeal to endure the disappointments, the hostility, the persecution, the martyrdom that have been met through the ages of mission history. Only God's power can account for the abiding results of missions—the groups of individuals who are living in quiet piety and witness, at peace with God and serenely confident in a frustrating world.

If any period of history would test the cause of mission it is ours. Crumbling social orders and disrupting governments cause disillusionment with things of temporal origin that were considered beneficial in the past. Only the eternal will stand.

> Built on the Rock the Church doth stand,
> Even when steeples are falling;
> Crumbled have spires in every land,
> Bells still are chiming and calling;
> Calling the young and old to rest,
> But above all the soul distressed,
> Longing for rest everlasting.[1]

These days have driven the church back to the rock foundation of missions. With varying emphases in different periods, with a multitude of activities necessarily conducted in addition to evangelism, and with many nationalities and types of personalities par-

13

ticipating in the program, varying interpretations and different approaches are inevitable. Missions have become diversified. Certain aspects may have been emphasized at the expense of others till there was an unbalanced program or till one branch of missions was conducted as an end in itself. Realizing this, the missionaries and mission agencies have entered into a careful examination of mission thought and purpose. The Bible, always the foundation for Christian thought and life, has been the basis of their study.

The Bible has been called "a missionary book." Most casual readers recognize mission material in the Book of Acts, but may pass by other portions. The entire Bible is permeated with the thought of mission.

> Throughout the Bible God's thought and plan for the world's evangelization are everywhere in evidence. From cover to cover the Bible is a missionary book, so much so that, as someone has expressed it, one cannot cut out its missionary significance without completely destroying the book.[2]

One of the key passages in the Bible is, "For God so loved the world that he gave his only Son, that whoever believes in him should not perish but have eternal life" (John 3:16).

The Old Testament is not merely a history of man up to the time of the New Testament. It is a history of God's dealings with man and nations. In each book one may see the unfolding of God's plan of salvation for man—which is mission in the deepest sense.

Interpretation of the Bible in light of *Heilsgeschichte* (history of salvation) was for many years held in contempt by certain Bible critics who were more interested in proving the religious dependence of Israel on their neighboring nations than in seeing Israel's influence on the nations, through God's revelation to them. Most of today's outstanding biblical scholars, among them Von Rad, are returning more and more to the concept that mission is embedded in the warp and woof of the Old Testament.

> The Old Testament historical work whose theological tendency we can most easily grasp is the Deuteronomistic history. If we question it—especially the two books of Kings—as to its purpose, that is, as to what theological concern this exilic historical school had, the concept of a "history of faith" is at once excluded, while that of a cult—or temple—history is seen to be equally inappropriate. Rather, one sees that what is given here is a his-

tory of the creative Word of God, that is, a course of history is described which is determined by a whole pattern of mutually corresponding prophetic promises and divine fulfillments. What interests these historians is the precise functioning in history of the Word as proclaimed by the prophets. In a positively classical manner the concept of *Heilsgeschichte* is here sketched as a course of history which is kept in motion, and guided to its God-ordained goal, by the constantly intruding divine Word.[3]

This concept is likewise evident in the New Testament where it constitutes the fulfillment of the history of salvation, begun in the Old Testament, centered in Christ.

> By naming the witnesses, the church points not only to an event in the past, but also to the consistent tradition of the salvific event, to the church itself as a factor of the *Heilsgeschichte*. Its self-consciousness is a historical one from the beginning.[4]

For some time it has been popular to start a study of the Old Testament with Moses, or with Abraham, so that the idea of the covenant people, Israel, can be the center of study. There is no doubt that the covenant concept illumines the whole history of the people of Israel. However, the question is raised as to whether there was no covenant of God with man before this time. Johannes Blauw begins his study of mission in the Old Testament with the first chapters of Genesis,

> It is no coincidence that the Old Testament has been handed down to us in its present form. The *arrangement, the order of the material,* also belongs to the kerygma, the message of the Old Testament. . . . The first chapters of Genesis are (as the whole book of Genesis, for that matter) a key to the understanding of all the rest of the Old Testament and even, for those who recognize the unity of the Bible, the whole Bible. . . . The first chapters of Genesis must therefore be seen also as witness, as confession concerning the *pre*-history of Israel as the People of God, and at the same time as *pre*-history which gives meaning to the history of Israel itself.[5]

But speaking of it as "pre-history" does not mean that what is in the early chapters of Genesis is embryonic form stuff from which a later development of man's theology could form a concept of a covenant with God through his redemptive action.

The theological and history-of-salvation views are joined together and bridge the Bible, from the first chapter of Genesis
to the last chapter of Revelation. There is a "line of salvation
with dual activity" with the two principles, selection and mediation; a minority is elected to bear and apply the blessing to
the benefit of the large whole.[6]

This is the plan of mission as it unfolds in the early chapters of
Genesis. But the story of mission begins with the creation of man,
as this initiates God's dealing with man for his salvation. Von Rad,
dealing with the creation story in Genesis, chapters one and two,
notes:

Direct theological statements about the Creation in the form of
large complexes occur only twice in the Old Testament . . .
precisely in those two sections where Creation is expressly intended to be understood as a prologue, and as a start of the
divine saving work in Israel.[7]

In other words, the story of creation in the Bible has a "soteriologi-
cal meaning." Blauw puts it in other words, declaring that the story
of creation is "not a philosophical or cosmological theory; it is simply the background to the human story, God's love story with the
human race."[8]

The great truth for man is that he is created of God and has a
special relationship to God. People do not live unto themselves or
in dependence upon any other power within earth. "Heredity did
not make them; environment did not make them; education did not
make them; God made them."[9] As the creatures of God they possess
a special nobility. God can reveal himself to man, and man can
respond. The relationship is to be maintained on this high level,
but there is also another aspect that is inherent in the fact of God
as Creator. The account in Genesis is detailed in order that both
the nobility of man born in the image of God, and his dependence
on God may be clearly seen.

It is in particular in the picture of creation of man and woman
that this account (in Genesis) is fully detailed and bold in its
vividness, for it depicts God the creator as completely applied
to his creation—without the slightest reserve, and occupied in
shaping it like a potter. The material utilized is the ground—
but man became a "living being" only by God's breathing into
him his own divine breath from his own mouth . . . Life is pos-

sessed by man only in virtue of that breath of God; and this
latter is in no sense inherently associated with his body, and
any withholding of this ephemeral gift would throw man back
to a state of dead matter.[10]

Man is truly *man*, in the full sense of that word, only in his relationship with God—in his dependence upon him as his Creator.
It is precisely against this relationship of dependence that man
rebelled. In the story of the fall into sin, man is seeking to elevate
himself "to be like God" (Gen. 3:5). This is the first of such rebel-
lions described in the first eleven chapters of Genesis. Cain replaced
God as judge over his brother with right to determine life and death.
The story of the period preceding the flood pictures men as living
godless lives—lives in which there was no room for the God-man
relationship of creation. The building of the Tower of Babel
showed an economic or racial Titanism whereby God was replaced.
Man, having lost his sense of dependence on God, looked upon himself as a corporate body living unto itself alone.

These sins may be found in our day, as they were repeatedly
found in the history of Israel, and among other people of the earth
in Old Testament times. History repeats itself. This is not mere history, but God's relationship to people and to nations *in* this kind of
history. God's hand is seen in judgment but also in a redemptive
covenant. This is true in each case.

Adam and Eve were excluded from the garden and constant fellowship with God, and lost the natural fellowship as God's creatures with one another. God gave a promise for the future, that
the head of the serpent would be crushed. He clothed man and
woman that their fellowship, by his act, would continue without
the shame that their sin brought into their relationship with one
another. Cain became an outcast, but with a mark that would, at
the same time, remind him of his sinful nature and assure protection against the hand of those who would seek to avenge him. To
Adam and Eve God gave Seth, who should continue the godly seed
upon earth. The flood came as judgment upon godlessness, but Noah
and his sons were chosen by God to rebuild his family on earth.

The incident of the Tower of Babel resulted in the scattering of
man in the world and the shattering of the image of man's reliance
on his own strength and resources. Man's faith in something outside himself—in God—was restored when God selected Abraham to

be the father of the "chosen people" of Israel, with the promise, "in you all the families of the earth shall be blessed" (Gen. 12:3).

The pattern of God's mission among the people was set. The aim was "a people holy unto God." God's method of achieving the goal is clear. Through judgment and mercy he appointed those who should be mediators between God and man. By life and oral witness they were "to bear and apply the blessing" from God to the people of the world.

This pattern is seen clearly in the history of Abraham, through the time of Moses and Joshua, and in the period of the kings. This section of Old Testament history possibly gives the best illustration of God's dealings with man. God's message of salvation was to be preserved and proclaimed by Israel, his chosen instrument. There were lapses in the keeping of the covenant that God established with Israel which were both serious and lengthy. There were long periods when Israel's mission was forgotten and was replaced with a nationalistic, self-centered, spiritual pride. There were times when God had to deal with Israel as he had dealt with the nations earlier. Those who showed disbelief and strayed from God in the wilderness journey from Egypt to Canaan were permitted to die in the desert. Because of disobedience to God, there were severe losses during the conquest of the promised land. The ten tribes of the northern kingdom were lost. Only a remnant of the southern kingdom was restored to Jerusalem after captivity. It is a long history of a blending of judgment and mercy. It is not a story of lives ethically perfect or of a people faithfully following a consuming mission. It can, however, be understood—in all its glory and sordidness—as a message of God, dealing with the nations, not just one particular nation.

> The call of Abraham, and the history of Israel which begins at that point, is the beginning of the restoration of the lost unity of mankind and of the broken fellowship with God. "In you all the families of the earth will be blessed" [or, "will bless themselves"], Gen. 12:3. Here it becomes clear that the whole history of Israel is nothing but the continuation of God's dealings with the nations, and that therefore the history of Israel is only to be understood from the unsolved problem of the relation of God to the nations.[11]

We cannot see the election of Israel as the covenant people of God aside from their missionary purpose. The two aspects of this act of God are evident: (1) the election and (2) the mediation or mission of Israel.

There is a technical expression used in reference to God's call to Abraham. "God caused me to wander from my father's house" (Ex. 20:13). "A wandering Aramean was my father; and he went down into Egypt and sojourned there, few in number; and there he became a nation, great, mighty, and populous" (Deut. 26:5). The term "wander from" (and "wandering") is used for sheep "gone astray" from the flock. The implication is "being destroyed" or "perishing." It is more easily translated in this way in other passages, as in Jeremiah, "My people have been lost sheep; their shepherds have led them astray" (Jer. 50:6). Here the situation carries a different connotation. Abraham was called away from the sheep among whom he was perishing so that he could become the leader of a new flock that was to be "the people of Yahweh."

God calls the people of Israel "my people" (Is. 3:12) and "a people holy to the Lord" (Jer. 2:3). The promises and acts of God on behalf of Israel indicated his presence with Israel in a special way, but salvation and its blessings belonged not only to Israel. God chose Israel that its people might be a blessing to the world, as indicated in the words of promise integrated in the call of Abraham. The term "holy" (*qadosh*) refers to consecration or dedication to God. The temple, the fittings of the temple, the priests in the temple were *qadosh*—dedicated to the service of God. Except when speaking of God, this is a relative term, always used in the sense of that which is consecrated for the use and glory of God.

This election meant that God was to be present and manifest in his people. The worship of Yahweh—the temple, the festival days, the sacrifices—were to remind them that God was in their midst. The law was given them so that under its tutelage they might be fit instruments to carry out God's purpose, conscious of their covenant relationship so that they would be a light to the Gentiles.

Old Testament law was never meant to be a constitutional law; the original Mosaic covenant was an order of freedom, freedom to live within the boundaries determined by the Lord, which were a denial of the right to serve other lords and the requirement of internal peace within the community. Judaism arose in the post-exilic period as a reform movement based on the collection of the variety of legal materials in an atmosphere of delayed eschatology, and their interpretation as the *Law* or constitution within which every step was to receive regulation. In the New Testament, Jesus and Paul revert to the older Israelite conception of the Covenant, jumping over, as it were, the Judaistic reformulation.[12]

Israel was a people consecrated to God for service, and he was present with them. This intimate union and fellowship of God's grace was to picture his love for people of all races.

Yahweh, as the name for God, was first introduced when he appeared before Moses. Moses wanted to know his name, and he replied, Yahweh—"I am who I am" (Ex. 3:14). Later he said to Moses, "I appeared to Abraham, to Isaac, and to Jacob, as God almighty, but by my name the Lord (Yahweh) I did not make myself known to them" (Ex. 6:3). However, he told Moses at that first meeting that he was the God of his fathers, and later mentioned that he (Yahweh) established his covenant with Abraham. It is difficult to give the exact meaning of the name "Yahweh," but it conveys action—that "he will be what he will be," to manifest himself in and through them. He is "a jealous God" (Ex. 34:14), "merciful and gracious, slow to anger and abounding in steadfast love and faithfulness" (Ex. 34:6).

As God of the fathers, he was with Abraham before the covenant relationship with him was established. It is also certain that he was known to the people among whom Abraham lived and from whom he was separated. There were remnants of true worshipers of God among nations outside of Israel. Revelation was not for Israel alone.

Abraham recognized Melchizedek as the priest of the true God and therefore higher than himself, and paid tithes to him.

> For this Melchizedek, king of Salem, priest of the Most High God, met Abraham returning from the slaughter of the kings and blessed him; and to him Abraham apportioned a tenth part of everything. He is first, by translation of his name, king of righteousness, and then he is also king of Salem, that is, king of peace. . . . But this man who has not their genealogy received tithes from Abraham and blessed him who had the promises. It is beyond dispute that the inferior is blessed by the superior (Heb. 7:1, 2, 6, 7).

There are other examples. Balaam, residing in Moab at the time of the exodus reluctantly blessed Israel before King Balek, saying "though Balek were to give me his house full of silver and gold, I could not go beyond the command of the Lord my God to do less or more." Rahab, the harlot who welcomed the spies that came to Jericho, confessed fear of Yahweh. Naaman's maid advised her pagan master to follow the advice of Elisha in order that he might be cured of his leprosy. Moses' father-in-law, a priest in Midian, was called as counselor of Moses, and was acquainted with the faith of the people of Israel.[13] Faith in God (whether he be called Elohim, Adonai, or Yahweh) was to be preserved by the people of Israel and was to be extended to others.

Among the special gifts to Israel for this purpose were the law, the established worship, God's special relevation to them, and his presence in their midst. The law cannot be understood apart from the covenant. Through this law they understood the holiness of God and also their responsibility to live as people of God in relationship to one another and to those who came in contact with them. They were taught to practice kindness to the wanderer, the slave, the underling, the widow, and the orphan. Those who joined their camp were under the same laws of justice as those born as people of Israel, and their personalities and property were equally protected.[14]

Their ritualistic form of worship was something quite different from pagan worship. They did not, through practice of ritual or magic, seek to get the attention of a god that they might coerce to do their will. The worship of Israel was basically a recounting of past acts of God on their behalf, with thanksgiving and prayer in recognition of their dependence on him.

The people of Israel recognized their special covenant relationship to God and their special relationship, *as the people of God,* to the world. Through the wilderness wanderings, and also in the new land of Canaan, they were ever mindful of God's dealing with mankind, the election out from the nations, and the mediation aspect—the mission—of this election.

> That it is God who joins this people to this land (Canaan) is not a subsequent historical interpretation of events: the wandering tribes themselves were inspired again and again in the promise made to their forefathers and the most enthusiastic among them saw God Himself leading His people into the promised land. It is impossible to imagine a historical Israel as existing at any time without belief in its God or previously

adhering to such a belief: . . . This belief in divine leadership is, however, at the same time the belief in a mission. . . . For these tribes divine leadership certainly implied an ordinance concerning the future in the land and from this basis a tradition and a doctrine were evolved. The story of Abraham, which connects the gift of Canaan with the command to be a blessing, is a most concise resume of the fact that the association of this people with the land signifies a mission. The people came to the land to fulfill the mission, even by each revolt against it they recognized its continuing validity; the prophets were appointed to interpret the past and future destiny of the people on the basis of its failure as yet to establish the righteous city of God for the establishment of which it had been led into the land. This land was at no time in the history of Israel simply the property of the people; it was always, at the same time, a challenge to make of it what God intended to have made of it.[15]

Through the turmoil and struggle of life that became the lot of Israel, and through contacts with pagan neighbors and the temptation to stray from Yahweh to other religions, and through developing their power as a kingdom on par with surrounding nations which based their hope of greatness on economic and military forces, Israel failed God in his purpose for them. As one reads the record of Israel, one is tempted to label it a "record of failures that ended in failure." But this history, replete as it is with stories of failure, reveals the hand of Yahweh as Lord of Israel and of the nations. Other nations testified again and again that they recognized that Yahweh was with his people, and confessed to the power of Yahweh as it was seen in and through Israel. Judges, kings, and prophets were God's special messengers to bring back the mission concept of the covenant to the people when they had lost it. That every nation is under God was one of the truths to be proclaimed by Israel.

And the One who is thus revealed is the God whose concern is the wholeness of life, life in its essential unity. For not only is all of life seen as "parts of His dominion," but all of these several parts are seen *together* as serving His purpose. This was the understanding of God given to the prophets of Israel. This was how they made sense of life, related religion to politics, gave meaning to history and hope to the world. For our storm-tossed generation it is the prophetic outlook that we need, the profound conviction which we have to recover—that history is not a tale full of sound and fury signifying nothing, but a record of the activity of God—and all this at the international as well as the personal level.[16]

Pagan, enemy nations were at times considered servants of God in judgment upon Israel or as places for Israel to continue her role as the missionary people of God.

Isaiah speaks of Israel in the same terms that would be used of a prophet under call, "But now hear, O Jacob my servant, . . . Thus says the Lord who made you, who formed you from the womb" (Is. 44:1-2). "Thus says the Lord to his anointed, to Cyrus . . . " (Is. 45:1). Israel is addressed as *ami* (my people) as over against the *goyim* (the nations); but though Israel has this distinction, she is also one of the *goyim*, and is treated as such. Righteousness is demanded of all nations, and all are under judgment as well as mercy. Amos, in his prophecy, dramatically shows how Judah, Israel, and the surrounding nations were used of God—one punishing the other when justice had failed.

David, in his closing message to the people, speaks of himself in the broader sense as ruler over men rather than as ruler over Israel. Solomon, in his prayer at the dedication of the temple, prays for blessing upon Israel. He closes with the words,

> Let these words of mine, wherewith I have made supplication before the Lord, be near to the Lord our God day and night, and may he maintain the cause of his servant, and the cause of his people Israel, as each day requires; *that all the peoples of the earth may know that the Lord is God;* there is no other. Let your heart therefore be wholly true to the Lord our God, walking in his statutes and keeping his commandments, as at this day (italics added) (1 Kings 8:59-61).

The Book of Jonah witnesses to the mission of Israel to other nations. This book is accepted by the Jews and considered by them to present the purpose of Yahweh. It shows that other nations are accountable to God, that they are sought by him, and that they can repent and turn to God in response to the proclamation of the prophet. Jonah was a prophet, a servant of God who went with some misgivings on a mission of evangelistic preaching to a non-Israelite people. When they repented they were spared the punishment they had been warned would come. God's mercy was on the "more than a hundred and twenty thousand *persons*" of Nineveh, though they were of a different race and culture (Jonah 4:11).

One concept of mission that persisted, through the period of Israel's life in Canaan and through the captivity of Judah into the time of the New Testament, was that God is Lord (literally "king") of all people, as he is Lord of creation. From the Psalms: "The Lord reigns; let the peoples tremble!" (Ps. 99:1). "The Mighty One, God the Lord, speaks and summons the earth" (Ps. 50:1). "Why do the nations conspire, and the people plot in vain? The kings of the earth set themselves, and the rulers take counsel together, against the Lord and his anointed, saying, 'Let us burst our bonds asunder, and cast their cords from us.' He who sits in the heavens laughs; the Lord has them in derision. Then he will speak to them in his wrath, and terrify them in his fury, saying, I have set my king on Zion, my holy hill" (Ps. 2:1-6).

From the prophets there are similar expressions:

> Lo, these shall come from afar, and lo, these from the north and from the west, and these from the land of Syene. Sing for joy, O heavens, and exult, O earth; break forth, O mountains, into singing! For the Lord has comforted his people, and will have compassion on his afflicted (Is. 49:12-13).

> How beautiful upon the mountains are the feet of him who brings good tidings, who publishes peace, who brings good tidings of good, who publishes salvation, who says to Zion, "Your God reigns" (Is. 52:7).

> I saw in the night visions, and behold, with the clouds of heaven there came one like a son of man, and he came to the Ancient of Days and was presented before him. And to him was given dominion and glory and kingdom, that all peoples, nations and languages should serve him; his dominion is an everlasting dominion, which shall not pass away, and his kingdom one that shall not be destroyed (Dan. 7:13-14).

The sovereign rule of Yahweh, in judgment, mercy, and justice, is an absolute reign that will tolerate no other ruler. The world is united under him. As God has established his rule in Israel, so will it be in all the world. The goal is that the covenant relationship of Israel be extended to the rest of the world—all peoples, all nations, under him. The passages speak of Yahweh as victorious king, able to pour his love and blessings unstintingly upon his people. All nature is in harmony, and man lives in blessed fellowship with God.

The centripetal nature of the kingdom is another Old Testament principle of mission, expressed vividly in Isaiah.

> It shall come to pass in the latter days that the mountain of the house of the Lord shall be established as the highest of the mountains, and shall be raised above the hills; and all nations shall flow to it, and many peoples shall come, and say: "Come, let us go up to the mountain of the Lord, to the house of the God of Jacob; that he may teach us his ways and that we may walk in his paths" (Is. 2:2-3).

> Arise, shine, for your light has come, and the glory of the Lord has risen upon you. For behold, darkness shall cover the earth, and thick darkness the peoples; but the Lord will arise upon you, and his glory will be seen upon you. And nations shall come to your light, and kings to the brightness of your rising. Lift up your eyes round about, and see; they all gather together, they come to you; your sons shall come from far, and your daughters shall be carried in the arms. Then you shall see and be radiant, your heart shall thrill and rejoice because the abundance of the sea shall be turned to you, the wealth of the nations shall come to you (Is. 60:1-5).

There are other portions of Scripture that point to the same divine power—the power of drawing people to Israel and its center in Zion. Zechariah depicts it graphically:

> Thus says the Lord of hosts: In those days ten men from the nations of every tongue shall take hold of the robe of a Jew, saying, "Let us go with you, for we have heard that God is with you" (Zech. 8:23).

It is difficult to interpret these passages without seeing the spirit of nationalism of Israel. It must be kept in mind that Hebrew was a language of pictures, and the people thought in figures of speech rather than in the logic of the Greek. It was the God of Abraham, Isaac, and Jacob who was to establish this universal rule. The glories of this rule were best expressed by an idealization of the past history of the people. Certainly the context implied that there was no longer a division between *am qadosh* and *goyim*. All were now the people of God and therefore all were become *am qadosh*.

Another factor that will aid in the interpretation is the New Testament use of this concept. Christ, speaking to the Jews, said, "I tell you, many will come from east and west and sit at table with

Abraham, Isaac, and Jacob in the kingdom of heaven" (Matt. 8:11-12). He also said, "and I, when I am lifted up from the earth will draw all men to myself" (John 12:32).

In those two passages we see the spiritual meaning of that which is presented in pictures in the Old Testament. The fulfillment gives meaning to the aspirations and aims of the past. The idea of Jesus as universal King is prominent in the New Testament, and the phrase "Jesus is King" was one of the early professions of the Christian faith. The Great Commission in Matthew's Gospel takes on new meaning when we consider it as the "marching orders" of Jesus the King to the children of the kingdom, rather than as a suggested objective placed before a few followers. "All authority in heaven and on earth has been given me. Go therefore . . . "

The universality of the kingdom, the messianic aspect of the kingdom, and its eschatological character are three Old Testament concepts that are intertwined.

> We are justified in concluding that the universal lordship of God, the eschatological expectation of salvation and the expectation of the Messiah belong together; they are, as it were, concentric circles: the Messiah is the centre of the Israelites as well as of the universal expectation of salvation.[17]

The universal kingdom was certainly thought of as taking place in history. But the future was also definitely involved and the messianic hope was the bridge to the future fulfillment of prophecy. When Jacob bade farewell to his sons he spoke prophetically,

> The scepter shall not depart from Judah, nor the ruler's staff from between his feet, until he comes to whom it belongs; and to him shall be the obedience of the peoples (Gen. 49:10).

The prophecy is continued in the words of Nathan to David:

> And your house and your kingdom shall be made sure forever before me; your throne shall be established forever (2 Sam. 7:16).

The theme of the kingdom was an important part in the worship of the people, as seen in the kingly Psalms.[18] It was the abiding hope and faith of the people of Israel in good and evil days alike, and was assured in the messages of the prophets.

In many places where reference is made to the messianic kingdom, in worship and prophecy, it is certain that it is to come through the missionary activity of Israel. In other places the *way* it is to come is not clearly indicated. In both instances the emphasis is on the act of God who established this kingdom in his own right and by his own power. Thus in prophecy it becomes a judgment on Israel and the other nations as well as a promise. It keeps the minds of the Israelites alert always to the fact that the present is not as it should be or as it one day will be. The promises of God are based on his presence as Lord of all the people.

> The people who walked in darkness have seen a great light; those who dwelt in a land of deep darkness, on them has the light shined. . . . For to us a child is born, to us a son is given; and the government will be upon his shoulder, and his name will be called "Wonderful Counselor, Mighty God, Everlasting Father, Prince of Peace." Of the increase of his government and of peace there will be no end, upon the throne of David, and over his kingdom, to establish it, and to uphold it with justice and with righteousness from this time forth and for evermore (Is. 9:2-6).

> And it shall come to pass in the latter days that the mountain of the house of the Lord shall be established . . . and people shall flow to it, and many nations shall come, and say: "Come, let us go up to the mountain of the Lord, to the house of the God of Jacob; that he may teach us his ways and that we may walk in his paths. For out of Zion shall go forth the law, and the word of the Lord from Jerusalem. He shall judge between many peoples, and shall decide for strong nations afar off; and they shall beat their swords into plowshares, and their spears into pruning hooks; nation shall not lift sword against nation, neither shall they learn war any more. . . . (Mic. 4:1-3).

> But you, O Bethlehem Ephrathah, who are little to be among the clans of Judah, from you shall come forth for me one who is to be ruler in Israel, whose origin is from of old, from ancient days. . . . And he shall stand and feed his flock in the strength of the Lord, in the majesty of the name of the Lord his God. And they shall dwell secure, for now he shall be great to the ends of the earth (Mic. 5:12-14).

> Behold, the days are coming, says the Lord, when I will raise up for David a righteous Branch, and he shall reign as king and deal wisely, and shall execute justice and righteousness in the land (Jer. 23:5).[19]

Many of these passages are directed specially toward the restoration of Israel as a nation under God, but they also have a broader messianic concept that points toward the fulfillment of God's desire to "draw all men," the entire world, unto himself. As the words of the covenant were never to be separated from the promise for all nations, Israel could never be without a sense of responsibility before God for the nations of the world. Karl Barth writes,

> Israel had and has a mission—that is the meaning of the covenant with it. In Israel—this is what will be revealed in the last days—there is to be set up a sign and a witness to all peoples. The redemptive will of God is to be declared to all humanity.[20]

There are four passages in Isaiah, called the "Songs of the Servant," that speak of Israel as the servant of the Lord. Like many prophecies, they point not only to the immediate, but also to the final fulfillment. These refer to the servant Israel and the servant Christ.

> The Servant is Israel, the whole community called to be a missionary community; the Servant is also the individual Jew who is called to make that mission his own, that through him it might be fulfilled; the Servant is also, and especially One Who should supremely in Himself embody that mission, and Who should carry it to a point no other should reach. That is to say, in so far as the Servant is an individual, He is not an individual in past history but One who lay in the future in the prophet's day.[21]

Many have called the Old Testament a missionary book, but equally many have said that Israel was not a missionary people. Perhaps it may be said that the New Testament, likewise, is a missionary book, but that few of those who claim to be followers of the Christ are missionaries. However, salvation for all people is the undying aim of God. As the people of Israel lived in righteousness and obedience to God they were blessed of him. It has been generally accepted that, by failing to be the missionary race God intended them to be, they lost their special covenant position. The task was transferred to the New Testament church—the messenger pointed to in prophecy—that was to bring the message of the Christ, the message of salvation to all peoples.

CHAPTER THREE

MISSION—BETWEEN
THE TESTAMENTS

A period of about four hundred years is covered by the term "between the Testaments." The term is not entirely correct, for there is some information in Scripture concerning the events of this period. One must go back to the Dispersion and the Babylonian Captivity of the Jews (587 B.C.) to get a proper background for the period. Between the Captivity and the time of Christ, a great change took place among the Jews. Their Jerusalem-centered worship had become, all but figuratively speaking, an impossibility. The exiles in Babylon were not the only Jewish people separated from their native land and traditional place of worship. There were large groups in Egypt and throughout areas of Persia, Arabia, and other lands of the Near East who continued faithful in the worship of Yahweh. The messianic prophecies of the later prophets became more meaningful to them. Their hope was still in Israel as the covenant people and they longed to return to Judea.

Two psalms (taking liberty with the date of composition of the second) illustrate the change in spirit of the Jews in reference to worship. When the Jews were taken captive and driven into exile in Babylon, they stopped at the border with dismay at the loss of their temple in Jerusalem. The possibility of worship seemed at an end.

By the waters of Babylon, there we sat down and wept, when we remembered Zion. On the willows there we hung up our lyres. For there our captors required of us songs, and our tormentors, mirth, saying, "Sing us one of the songs of Zion!" How shall we sing the Lord's song in a foreign land? (Ps. 137: 1-4).

29

But another psalm represents their spirit at the time of their return:

> When the Lord restored the fortunes of Zion, we were like those who dream. Then our mouth was filled with laughter, and our tongue with shouts of joy; then they said among the nations, "The Lord has done great things for them" (Ps. 126:1-2).

They had learned to "sing the Lord's song in a foreign land." Their vision had been broadened. God had been with them even when they were exiles and dwellers abroad. God had been worshiped even there. Those who could not return to Jerusalem continued to worship him in the land where they established residence.

Ezekiel was the missionary to the Diaspora in Babylon as Jeremiah was in Egypt. He was under commission of God who spoke to him:

> "Son of man, I send you to the people of Israel, to a nation of rebels, who have rebelled against me; they and their fathers have transgressed against me to this very day. The people also are impudent and stubborn: I send you to them; and you shall say to them, 'Thus says the Lord God' " (Ezek. 2:3-4).

He sought to bring them back into covenant relationship with God, though they were separated from the traditional setting of national Jewish worship. Many of the Jews in exile were living in their own homes in their own communities, many of them in business, leading lives comparatively free from the restraints usually associated with captivity. Ezekiel visited these people.

> In the sixth year, in the sixth month, on the fifth day of the month, as I sat in my house, with the elders of Judah sitting before me, the hand of the Lord God fell there upon me (Ezek. 8:1).

> In the seventh year, in the fifth month, on the tenth day of the month, certain of the elders of Israel came to inquire of the Lord, and sat before me. And the word of the Lord came to me: "Son of man, speak to the elders of Israel, and say to them, Thus says the Lord God, Is it to inquire of me that you come? As I live, says the Lord God, I will not be inquired of by you. Will you judge them, son of man, will you judge them? Then let them know the abominations of their fathers, and say to them, Thus says the Lord God: On the day when I chose Israel, I swore to the seed of the house of Jacob, making myself known to them in the land of Egypt, I swore to them, saying, I am the Lord your God" (Ezek. 20:1-5).

The people had organized and elected elders who came to Ezekiel to hear the Word of the Lord. The message that Ezekiel gave them was one of repentance. They were to repent for their own failure and, on behalf of the entire nation, for its past rebellion against God. With the promise of a new life and a new spirit given in the vision of the valley of dry bones (Ezek. 37) Ezekiel sought to rebuild the nation on the basis of the covenant promise. The Israelites learned to recognize that their captivity was not because God had deserted his people. It was rather punishment from God, proving his continued presence and his concern to rebuild them for his purpose. Ezekiel's message restored their faith in God as ruler of the nations, and in their own people as God's implement to make his will known. They recognized that they had failed as God's witnesses. They realized the importance of retaining their character as the people of God in the midst of the Gentiles.

There were two concrete developments resulting from this new faith and vision. One was the establishment of the synagogue; the other, a program of proselytizing.

The meeting of the elders with Ezekiel may have been the embryonic beginning of the synagogues that sprang up wherever there were Jews in sufficient numbers. Synagogues continued to be the religious centers in the time of Paul's active missionary work, and are to be found today in every land where there are Jews. Though religious practices were greatly simplified in comparison with the former worship in Jerusalem, the Word of God became precious to the people and knit them together in hope. There was new understanding of the need for this spiritual unity, and synagogues became the means of preserving the Israelites and also became the centers of witness.

The witness of the Jews was extensive. They were scattered into Babylon, Syria, Asia Minor, and other parts of the Tigris-Euphrates Valley, Egypt, and North Africa. Historians consider that about seven percent of the people in areas around the Mediterranean were Jews. Many pagan people became followers of the Jewish faith. The Jews had social and economic relations with the Gentiles among whom they lived. Their revitalized faith became evident. To maintain friendly understanding among these people, the Jews may have been forced to explain why they did not join in the pagan worship of the particular locality where they lived and had their business. This led to proclamation of their faith in Yahweh, the monotheistic God of Israel. Much of the literature was apologetic, a defense against anti-Jewish propaganda and feeling.

> The impulse of self-respect, the desire to be understood, the fear of economic and social disadvantage, all led the Jews to a literary campaign of self-defense. The aim was to show the antiquity of Judaism, its honorable position as the source of the philosophies of the Hellenistic world, the superiority of monotheism, the reasonableness and even surpassing greatness of many of the social provisions of the Mosaic law. . . . The defense of Judaism was necessarily an argument for it.[1]

Except in faith, the Jews conformed to the societies in which they lived. Their religion became crystallized as their one treasure that made them what they were—a race under the blessing of God with promises yet to be fulfilled. The Jews in many areas adopted the Greek language and culture. This was true especially in Egypt and in the elephantine area of Africa. The translation of the Septuagint for the use of the Hellenistic Jews made the Scripture available to all Greek-speaking people. The Scriptures became a missionary implement.

The extent of the success of proselytism cannot be ascribed only to a spirit of self-preservation or to an accidental development arising from lesser motives. The Jews had a new understanding of their role among the nations. There is evidence that the messianic concept of the kingdom of God with its emphasis on Yahweh as "Lord over the nations" became a stimulus to their witness.

> We cannot . . . give even an approximate count of the proselytes to Judaism in the Mediterranean world of the New Testament period. They were numerous enough to claim the attention of Philo and Josephus, conspicuous enough for pagan writers such as Tacitus and Horace and Juvenal to see them as a part of the Judaism of their time. They are looked upon as a factor in the great growth of the Jewish population following the Exile. The rapid development of Christianity into a Gentile religion seems inexplicable without a large proselyte constituency. More than this can hardly be said.[2]

This zeal was noted by Jesus when he said, "Woe to you, scribes and Pharisees, hypocrites! for you traverse sea and land to make a single proselyte, and when he becomes a proselyte you make him twice as much a child of hell as yourselves" (Matt. 23:15).

The greatest number of proselytes was reached by the Hellenists, possibly because, in their acceptance of Greek language and culture, they were less narrowly Jewish in their outlook and therefore less demanding of the people who became followers of the Jewish faith.

> Extensive and intensive recruiting for the Jewish faith was obviously undertaken by Hellenistic Jews. There the meaning of "proselytes" and the corresponding "God-fearers," was terminologically fixed. When this movement set in cannot be said for certain, but it was certainly well under way in the second century B.C.[3]

The proselyte was one who fully accepted the Jewish faith and observed Jewish laws, regulations, and rites, including circumcision. The God-fearer was one who acknowledged Yahweh as the only God, and followed the general ethical practices of Judaism. Such a man was Cornelius, described in Acts as "an upright and God-fearing man, who is well spoken of by the whole Jewish nation" (Acts 10:22). It is probable that the men of many nationalities who heard the Gospel on the day of Pentecost were of this latter group. Having been reached by the messages of Hellenistic Jews, they had assembled at the great festival in Jerusalem.

Some proselytism was carried out at a later date by the Palestinian Jews. They were more strict in demanding full adherence to laws, customs, and practices of the traditional Jewish religion. This work of the Palestinians is usually associated with Hillel.

The winning of converts to Judaism was often the natural result of witness by the people of Jewish faith in their particular localities. There was evidence of missionary work also being conducted on the basis that we usually speak of missions in our day, of someone being *sent* as a witness.

> There are prototypes of such activity in II Chronicles, as well as in II Maccabees. In the former it is stated that Jehoshaphat sent out "princes" and "Levites" with the law of the Lord to teach in the cities of Judah. . . . A dominant interest was the consolidation of the new community and the winning from the neighboring tribes of such as were friendly to the worship of Jehovah at Jerusalem. The passage from II Maccabees repre-

sents delegates being sent from Jerusalem to the Jews resident
in Alexandria, advising them of the time of the Feast of Taber-
nacles. A similar notice is found in Esther, where the Feast of
Purim is established and messages are sent to inform the communities.[4]

Proselytes (literally "believers away from the homeland") were
considered members of the covenant people. In some writings a
sharp distinction is drawn between the Jew-born-a-Jew and one
who had been accepted as a proselyte. The position of the Jew was
always higher, but the spiritual benefits were the same for both.
Philo reported that they all formed a "united fellowship" with no
distinction between them.

The Jews had many friends among the Gentiles besides those
who were won into their fellowship. It is probable that it was
such friends who united with the Jews in opposition to the preaching of Paul, on several occasions. It is also probable that many
Gentiles who became converts to Christ through Paul's preaching
were either God-fearers or friends of the Jews who regularly fre-
quented the synagogues.

There was a liberalization of the Jewish religion geographically,
culturally, and ethnologically, but not theologically. There is little
evidence of a strong eschatological vision among the Jews of the
Diaspora. The central driving force of their faith was in the messianic prophecies that would be fulfilled in history. They looked for
a glorified restoration of the past. The people of the nations would
come to faith in Yahweh *through* the blessing upon Israel. There
was a strong nationalistic feeling, common to immigrants who permanently reside in countries other than their own. (The idealized
picture of the motherland, as it was in the past, is retained and
handed down to future generations. In many ways, the immigrants
become more conservative, as they look back to the mother country, than the people who remain there and look to the future.)
This spirit kept them from proclaiming God in spiritual freedom,
without clothing the message in Jewish garb.

CHAPTER FOUR

THE GOSPELS AND MISSION

Mission, preeminently a revelation of God to the people, is initiated and continued as God's self-revelation in the New Testament. Proclamation is by man, but it is God who speaks through him, and it is God who reveals himself in history and, in mercy, receives man to himself. Mission begins in the New Testament with a new and fuller revelation of God.

> In the beginning was the Word, and the Word was with God, and the Word was God. He was in the beginning with God; all things were made through him, and without him was not anything made that was made. In him was life, and the life was the light of men. . . . And the Word became flesh and dwelt among us, full of grace and truth; we have beheld his glory, glory as of the only Son from the Father. . . . No one has ever seen God; the only Son, who is in the bosom of the Father, he has made him known (John 1:1-4, 14, 18).

Man is to face God directly in Jesus Christ. Tradition and the many regulations for life and worship in the Old Testament were to lead man to God. Now God meets man directly in his Son. Every man is on the same plane as he stands before his Creator and Redeemer. Jeremiah had foreseen this day when he prophesied:

> "Behold, the days are coming, says the Lord, when I will make a new covenant with the house of Israel and the house of Judah, not like the covenant which I made with their fathers when I took them by the hand to bring them out of the land of Egypt, my covenant which they broke, though I was their husband, says the Lord. But this is the covenant which I will make with

> the house of Israel after those days, says the Lord: I will put
> my law within them, and I will write it upon their hearts; and
> I will be their God, and they shall be my people. And no longer
> shall each man teach his neighbor and each his brother, saying,
> 'Know the Lord,' for they shall all know me, from the least of
> them to the greatest, says the Lord; for I will forgive their iniq-
> uity and I will remember their sin no more" (Jer. 31:31-34).

The new covenant is the covenant of grace in which each individual, through the new revelation, may know the Lord and live
in him.

The Great Commission given to the disciples to proclaim the
Gospel to all people is also new. Some commentators (among them
Ferdinand Hahn) say that there was no real sense of missions in
the Old Testament times or in the time between the Testaments
because the people were not then under a direct commission. In one
sense this was true, but certainly such a commission was implied
in the covenant relationship of the people with Yahweh, the Creator and King of all the world. In the New Testament we see the
crystallization of this *implied* mission whereby the church becomes
the designated instrument in God's hand for carrying out his purpose.

The expectations of the Old Testament are more than fulfilled—
they are exceeded in the revelation of the Son. At the same time,

> the "new" in the New Testament is nothing else than that
> which had already been predicted in the Old Testament, and it
> is of great significance that the "new" in the New Testament
> is illuminated and clarified time and again from the Old Testa-
> ment.[1]

There is continuity, but not identity. In the New Testament the
idea of the Davidic kingdom is found, but it does not include the
Jewish concept of a glorious earthly kingdom. Isaiah's concept of
the suffering servant is presented graphically in the Christ who
was hated, reviled, and crucified.

> The essential absolutely unique feature in the revelation of God
> in Christ is that, contrary to all human conceptions, God's reve-
> lation is an offense to man. . . . Revelation in Christ is a free
> divine act of redemptive irruption into the life of man and of
> the world. This is an offense to man, because all philosophy, all
> idealistic religion, all consistent mystical religion, all moralism

meet in one point. They constitute various endeavors for self-redemption, and instinctively reject the truth that God and God alone can work redemption.[2]

Christ personifies mission. God's love for all mankind is manifest in Christ, and it is in him alone that salvation is offered to the world. This revelation of God in Christ demands a response from man. No one can be indifferent. Man either accepts or rejects. Christ is both Judge and Savior. Seeming perfection in keeping the law, and the elaborate ritualistic practices of the Jews are condemned for hiding God rather than revealing him. The actions and efforts of man in other religions are a substitute for God rather than a road to God. In Christianity man is stripped of his own "goodness" to see his utter and total dependence upon God. Salvation is by grace. Christ does not come to lead people into a gradually-developing paradise, but to create a new heart *within* them. "We evangelize men and women, *not* situations, *not* humanity, *not* abstractions of any kind but only flesh and blood."[3] The Jew, Greek, Egyptian, Mesopotamian, and Roman all stand before God on the same basis. All are members of the human race, equally in need of mercy. For all, God is concerned. This universal need for salvation is the key to the mission message of the New Testament.

The history of God's salvation reaches its climactic fulfillment in the Gospels. It is in Christ that the prophetic utterances of the Old Testament are fully understood.

> Therefore the Lord himself will give you a sign. Behold, a young woman (virgin) shall conceive and bear a son, and shall call his name Immanuel (Is. 7:14).

> For to us a child is born, to us a son is given; and the government will be upon his shoulder, and his name will be called "Wonderful Counselor, Mighty God, Everlasting Father, Prince of Peace." Of the increase of his government and of peace there will be no end, upon the throne of David, and over his kingdom, to establish it, and to uphold it with justice and with righteousness from this time forth and for evermore (Is. 9:6-7).

> Behold my servant, whom I uphold, my chosen, in whom my soul delights; I have put my Spirit upon him, he will bring forth justice to the nations. He will not cry nor lift up his voice, or make it heard in the street; a bruised reed he will not break, and a dimly burning wick he will not quench; he will faithfully bring forth justice. He will not fail or be discouraged

> till he has established justice in the earth; and the coastlands wait for his law (Is. 42:1-4).

> It is too light a thing that you should be my servant to raise up the tribes of Jacob and to restore the preserved of Israel; I will give you as a light to the nations, that my salvation may reach to the end of the earth (Is. 49:6).

> The Spirit of the Lord God is upon me, because the Lord has anointed me to bring good tidings to the afflicted; he has sent me to bind up the broken-hearted, to proclaim liberty to the captives, and the opening of the prison to those who are bound; to proclaim the year of the Lord's favor, and the day of vengeance of our God (Is. 61:1-2).

These passages from Isaiah that refer to Jesus are quoted in the first chapters of Luke's Gospel.[4] When Jesus, in Nazareth, announced his ministry he quoted Isaiah 61:1-2a, and proclaimed, "today this scripture has been fulfilled in your hearing" (Luke 4:21).

Regulations of the law were observed in the early life of Jesus in his circumcision and his presentation at the temple. He frequently quoted the Old Testament. "Think not that I have come to abolish the law and the prophets; I have come not to abolish them but to fulfill them" (Matt. 5:17). He acknowledged his special responsibility to the people of Israel.

> There is no doubt that Jesus directed his work in the first place to Israel. He laid claim to God's people as a whole. In this he followed John the Baptist, who likewise addressed himself to all Israel, summoned them to repentance, and warned them of God's judgment. But whereas John's ministry was dominated by the preaching of judgment, Jesus was concerned with a great new promise of salvation. He did not turn back to the idea of gathering the holy remnant, as was the widespread tendency in the Judaism of that time, but took up again the Old Testament concept of God's people.[5]

He was concerned that their faith might be freed from the extraneous, man-made laws that had been added to their worship, and be purified so that the individual would trust solely in Yahweh for salvation. He also sought to create in them the mission concept and purpose of their special relationship to God in the covenant. It was necessary to broaden their vision to see that salvation was for all people, to accept Christ as "the Messiah" who was to come: and the messianic kingdom as a universal spiritual kingdom. Jesus attacked the scribes and Pharisees as hypocrites, who had perverted the message of God and had led others into the same error.[6] The frequent examples in the Old Testament of God's blessings upon non-Israelites and the warnings that God's judgment would be heavier upon the Israelites than upon pagan cities[7] were given to awaken the people to know that personal relationship to God must be established *through him*, that the kingdom was for all people, including the Jews.

The "kingdom of God" was a concept familiar to the Jews as a kingdom that was to come some time in the future. Jesus spoke of the kingdom as being "at hand" and dealt with it in an eschatological sense. The eschatology had a dual aspect referring both to the "now" and the "future." Christ's coming was eschatological. His followers lived in the kingdom of the "now" but looked forward to the time of his return when all creation would know him as King and when he would create the new heaven and the new earth and rule forevermore. The future aspect did not eliminate the "now" of the kingdom. John the Baptist preached, "Repent, for the kingdom of heaven is at hand" (Matt. 3:2). Jesus began his ministry in Galilee, "preaching the gospel of God, and saying, 'The time is fulfilled, and the kingdom of God is at hand; repent and believe in the gospel' " (Mark 1:14-15).

Jesus sent the twelve apostles out "to preach the kingdom of God" (Luke 9:2). When he sent the seventy out, the instruction was, "say to them, 'The kingdom of God has come near you' " (Luke 10:9). This was the mission preaching of that time. There was no ambiguity in the message: "Repent" (literally, "have a change of mind"), "Believe in the gospel," "Leave what you are vainly following and enter the kingdom of God by me." Jesus said of himself, "I am the way, and the truth, and the life; no one comes to the Father, but by me" (John 14:6). "The kingdom of God is not coming with signs to be observed; nor will they say, 'Lo, here it is!' or 'There!' for behold, the kingdom of God is in the midst of you" (Luke 17:20-21). Jesus said to his followers, "Fear not, little flock, for it is your Father's good pleasure to give you the kingdom" (Luke 12:32). "The law and the prophets were until John; since then the good news of the kingdom of God is preached, and every one enters it violently" (Luke 16:16).

The direct, active missionary work of Jesus in "spreading the Way" has been debated by New Testament scholars. Some have placed emphasis on the founding of the kingdom for future mission activity, others on the personal mission activity of Jesus. Adolph Harnack declares that the idea of mission was foreign to the preaching of Jesus, and that world missions could not have been within the horizon of his vision.[8] This attitude presupposes that Jesus saw the kingdom only as a restoration of the people of the Old Testament Covenant, with missions being left to the future. Jesus sought to draw the Jews unto *himself* in faith, but mission, in the sense of reaching out beyond the Jews, was also inherent in both his work and preaching.

Matthew makes a clear distinction between "teaching the law" and the "preaching of the Gospel," in order to emphasize the missionary aspect of Christ and those sent out by him "with authority" to preach the Gospel to Gentiles and Jews alike. The synoptic Gospels tell of Jesus *first* going to the Jews, but because of their rejection or hardness of heart, *later* going to the Gentiles.

Much of the ministry of Jesus was in Galilee, and considerable effort was made to reach the Samaritans. Mark tells of Jesus going to the "region of Tyre and Sidon," healing the daughter of a Greek woman, and curing a man in Decapolis who had an "impediment in his speech." Luke deals at great length with Christ's ministry in Galilee following his statement, "I must preach the good news of the kingdom of God to the other cities also; for I was sent for this purpose" (Luke 4:43).

Luke later reports that Pharisees and teachers of the law had come to hear him from "every town in Galilee" as well as from Judea and Jerusalem. The Jewish leaders, because of their argument with Jesus, were specifically mentioned, but the rest of the crowd there and most of the 5,000 and 4,000 who were fed by the Sea of Gennesaret were certainly local people who were not considered Jews. His efforts to reach the Samaritans can be seen from the incident at the well where Jesus conversed with "a woman of Samaria." She not only believed that he was the Christ, but she witnessed of him to the city of Sychar. "Many Samaritans from that city believed in him because of the woman's testimony . . . and he stayed two days. And many more believed because of his word. They said to the woman, 'It is no longer because of your words that we believe, for we have heard for ourselves, and we know that this is indeed the Savior of the world'" (John 4:39-42). On his way to Jerusalem, Jesus sent disciples before him into Samaria to prepare for his coming. His parable of the Good Samaritan shows his attitude to the Samaritans, and was a rebuke to the Jews for the lack of living manifestation of faith among them.[9]

Besides his direct ministry among the Gentiles, Jesus sought to open the eyes of the Jews to the universality of God's salvation and judgment, and to their historic role as a missionary people.

1. At the last judgment Israel as well as all the nations, will stand before God. Matt. 25:31 ff.; 8:11-12; 12:41 ff.

2. The promises of the covenant are no guarantee against the judgment of God. Matt. 3:9; Luke 13:6-9.

3. The differences between Israel and the "nations" will fall away. Matt. 23:37; Luke 13:1-3.

4. The term "son of man" that he uses of himself refers back to Daniel 7:13-14 where the Messiah is presented as ruler of *all* peoples and nations—in an everlasting dominion.

5. His death is for all men. Matt. 15:21; Mark 10:45; 14:24.

In the parables of Jesus that refer especially to the coming and nature of the kingdom, the teaching of the outreached hand of God to all peoples, irrespective of race, is found. The parables of "The Sower," "Tares Among the Wheat," "The Net," and "The Mustard Seed" in the thirteenth chapter of Matthew and of "The Lost Sheep," "The Lost Coin," and "The Prodigal Son" in the fifteenth of Luke, all have universal rather than Jewish implications. One cannot accept these parables and the direct admonitions of Jesus without realizing the missionary character of the kingdom that he established.

Both Jews and Gentiles were drawn to Jesus. It was from among the Jews that he selected his apostles. The Roman centurion who asked Jesus to heal his servant was most likely a God-fearer who had been reached earlier by the proselyting Jews. He was not a Jew, nor recognized as a proselyte, but the Jews said of him, "He is worthy to have you do this for him, for he loves our nation, and he built us a synagogue." Of him Jesus said, "I tell you, not even in Israel have I found such faith."

There was also the official in Capernaum who came to Jesus requesting him to heal his son.[10] There were the Greeks who came to Philip with the plea, "Sir, we would see Jesus." From the reports of his preaching missions in Judea, Galilee, Samaria, and the border regions, it is evident that there were larger or smaller groups in each area who accepted Christ as the Savior. Paul wrote that after appearing to the few following his resurrection, "He appeared to more than five hundred brethren at one time" (1 Cor. 15:6). How many there were who came as direct result of the preaching and personal witness of Jesus, the "Twelve," and the "Seventy," and others is not known. They were the forerunners of the multitudes to be led to Christ by similar witness of Christians in succeeding generations.

When Jesus sent the Twelve and the Seventy out to preach, he gave them the power and authority to use the same methods that he used—to proclaim that the kingdom was at hand, to heal the sick and raise the dead. There is no indication that the ministry of healing was exercised as an end in itself to win disciples. Miracles were performed to establish the authority of the Word that was preached, and to manifest the nature of the kingdom. The admonition was "to *preach* [proclaim] the kingdom of God and to heal." Matthew, using the term "preach" in connection with "the gospel," more definitely emphasized the missionary nature of their proclamation. Mark, in his account of the missionary journey of the Twelve, said, "So they went out and preached that men should repent."[11] Here is the key to the missionary message—the kingdom of heaven is at hand; man is to turn, away from his vain worship, to Christ.

Other detailed instructions were given by Jesus to those sent out on the early evangelistic trips. They should take nothing with them, but should be totally dependent on the people they ministered to for their own sustenance, for travel arrangements, and for places of assembly. In order to establish a Christian center in a community, they should stay at one place and not move about from house to house. To the Seventy there was a special directive which must also have applied to the Twelve. Jesus said, "Whatever house you enter, first say, 'Peace be to this house!' And if a son of peace is there, your peace shall rest upon him; but if not it shall return to you" (Luke 10:5-6). Their dependence upon the people shows the spirit of hospitality in those days, and also shows the receptivity of people to the Gospel and its messengers. The disciples offered something that was of blessing. When accepted, the apostles were brought immediately into a family relationship with the converts who, from the beginning, shared in the work of evangelism. The "peace" wished upon the house had the background and deeper meaning of the Old Testament *"shalom,"*

> which denotes salvation in the comprehensive sense; moreover, the peace greeting is understood as an effective utterance and therefore, in certain cases, the saving power that goes to people can return to the messenger. But now on the lips of Jesus' messengers, such a peace greeting is subsumed under the proclamation of God's Kingdom, whence it receives meaning and strength.[12]

Their task was one of proclamation, and of building centers that should serve as places of worship and points of continued witness to the community.

The foundation of the kingdom was laid in the life and death of Jesus, in his work of witness, and in his resurrection. The establishment of this kingdom by the disciples after the resurrection, the missionary program of the church, was dependent on the Holy Spirit who prepared and equipped the disciples for the dramatic continuation of that which Jesus had begun. The gift of the Spirit, which had not yet been given "because Jesus was not yet glorified," was necessary for the proclamation of the Gospel.

> Nevertheless I tell you the truth; it is to your advantage that I go away, for if I do not go away, the Counselor will not come to you; but if I go, I will send him to you. And when he comes, he will convince the world of sin and of righteousness and of judgment; of sin because they do not believe in me; of righteousness, because I go to the Father, and you will see me no more; of judgment, because the ruler of this world is judged (John 16:7-11).

> But when the Counselor comes, whom I shall send to you from the Father, even the Spirit of truth, who proceeds from the Father, he will bear witness to me; and you also are witnesses, because you have been with me from the beginning (John 15:26-27).

> But you shall receive power when the Holy Spirit has come upon you; and you shall be my witnesses in Jerusalem and in all Judea and Samaria and to the end of the earth (Acts 1:8).

This is the equipment for the missionary outreach of the church. The Spirit convicts the listener of sin and reveals his need for salvation that Christ alone provides.

This is the answer to the longing void in the hearts of men who so frequently are led astray to false gods. When Moses was on Mt. Sinai and the people had grown weary of waiting for his return, Aaron answered their cry, "Make us gods, who shall go before us." The history of mankind has been a history of rebellion against God. Man has made God into man's own image. This image may be a primitive idol, modern materialism, or any influence that enslaves man in his own creations. Before these idols Christ stands as the liberator. Through the Spirit, Christ says " . . . you will know the truth, and the truth will make you free. . . . So if the Son makes you free, you will be free indeed" (John 8:32, 36).

Christ's role in the development of mission cannot be fully understood outside this plan revealed by him for the extension of the kingdom. The eschatological aspect in the missionary message was demonstrated and actualized in the death, resurrection, and ascension of Christ, and applied through the giving of the Holy Spirit. Oscar Cullmann speaks of this aspect of the missionary message in reference to the royal sovereignty of Christ. It will be continued until Christ "delivers the kingdom to God the Father after destroying every rule and every authority and every power" (1 Cor. 15:24).

> Under the impulse of the Holy Spirit the eschatological summons to action: "Repent!" is seen in the right light. It is because the kingdom has come nearer to us, and, in the Holy Spirit, is, in part, already here, that it is now possible for us to act in a Christian way.

> It is the presence of the Holy Spirit which makes the action of the Church, as such, eschatological. The Church itself is an eschatological phenomenon. It is the center of the present Lordship of Christ. It was constituted by the Holy Spirit at Pentecost.[13]

With the promise of the Holy Spirit given, Christ gave the Great Commission to his disciples, as found in Matthew 28:19-20.

> Go therefore and make disciples of all nations, baptizing them in the name of the Father and of the Son and of the Holy Spirit, teaching them to observe all that I have commanded you; and lo, I am with you always, to the end of the age.

Some literary critics have recently claimed that this Great Commission is a later editorial addition to the Gospel. Others have defended it because it does not stand alone. Surely it breathes the very spirit of the Gospels. It is a natural and fitting conclusion to the ministry of Jesus and gives meaning to the equipment that is to be given to the disciples in the Holy Spirit. Though in varying forms, the commission is substantially the same in all Gospels.[14] Blauw calls attention to the striking fact that the Great Commission is given in the Synoptic Gospels and the Gospel of John as a culmination of Christ's resurrection.[15] Dr. Karl Barth states,

> It was during this period that the purpose of Jesus' life and death, and with it the mission of his followers, could for the first time be seen, heard, and grasped by men. . . . He appeared to them not in order to continue his ministry of teaching and healing, so to speak, during the second part of his earthly life, but to disclose the hitherto hidden purpose of his life and death to his followers and to give them the charge of proclaiming his Lordship and the kingdom now manifest before their eyes.[16]

The "Great Commission" as given in Matthew gives the kingdom concept its highest spiritual sense. The kingdom is not all men, but it is for all men. The responsibilities are delegated to man, but man stands in partner-relationship with God, under the Holy Spirit. Each Christian is a participant in the blessings of the kingdom. Each Christian, through his witness, is an active participant in the building of the kingdom. Christ ushered in the new missionary era that began with the apostles and will continue until Christ's return.

CHAPTER FIVE

MISSION IN THE APOSTOLIC AGE

Immediately after commissioning the disciples to witness to all the world, Christ told them to wait in Jerusalem till they were "clothed with power from on high" (Luke 24:49). As the disciples, obedient to the admonition, were waiting, the promise was fulfilled. The Holy Spirit was given by God, to show people their need of a Savior, to call them to the Christ, and to equip them for witness. The mission era, for the apostles and for the church, began with Pentecost. The apostles had a message to give and they were endowed with the power to witness—this made them missionaries.

A prophetic utterance by Joel, quoted by Peter, describes the day in which we live, a period ushered in by the Apostolic Age:

> And in the last days it shall be, God declares, that I will pour out my spirit upon all flesh, and your sons and your daughters shall prophesy, and your young men shall see visions, and your old men shall dream dreams; yea, and on my menservants and my maidservants in those days I will pour out my Spirit; and they shall prophesy. And I will show wonders in the heaven above and signs on the earth beneath, blood, and fire, and vapor of smoke; the sun shall be turned into darkness and the moon into blood, before the day of the Lord comes, the great and manifest day. And it shall be that whoever calls on the name of the Lord will be saved (Acts 2:17-21).

This period is sometimes spoken of as "the fullness of time"—the time made ready by God for the Christ and for his true spiritual kingdom on earth. There were some external conditions in the political, cultural, and religious world at that time that were favorable to the expansion of Christianity. Harnack lists the following:

1. The spread of Judaism that brought the idea of monotheism to people of other cultures and also provided natural contact with the apostles of Jesus.

2. Hellenization of the East had created a comparative unity of language and ideas that could become a tool for transmission of the Gospel message.

3. The Roman Empire had secured political unity for the nations around the Mediterranean. Its laws were considered a safeguard and shelter. The emperor was looked upon as a symbol of peace.

4. International traffic and good means of communication had widened the intercourse of peoples and nations.

5. Practical and theoretical convictions of the essential unity of mankind, human rights, and duties were established. Christians in most instances could assent to them.

6. The decomposition of ancient society and formation of a democracy gradually equalized the Roman cities of Greeks and Barbarians and the various classes of society.

7. The tolerant policy of Rome furthered interchange of religions.

8. Eruption of Syrian and Persian religions into the empire, at first a handicap to Christianity, stirred religious cravings among the people.

9. Popularization of knowledge and rising interest in the mystical philosophies of religion kindled a craving for some form of revelation and a thirst for miracle.

The narrow world had become a wide world; the rent world had become a unity; the barbarian world had become Greek and Roman: *One* empire, *one* universal language, *one* civilization, a *common* development towards monotheism, and a *common yearning* for saviors.[1]

The factors in the world situation that contributed to the spread of Christianity must be noted, but should not be overemphasized. Christianity met with a great deal of opposition at the time of the apostles, but the number of Christians increased in spite of government bans and religious and government persecution.

Pentecost has frequently been called the birthday of the church. The message given by the apostles in Jerusalem on that day was the same as that given when they had been sent out by Christ on their earlier preaching missions—"repent and believe." It was the proclamation of the Gospel, the lordship of God over all the nations, the love of God for all people. They referred to the Old Testament history and prophecies as the revelation of God, pointing to their day, showing that the crucified and risen Jesus was indeed the Christ. The results of the preaching among the listeners was immediate.

> Now when they heard this they were cut to the heart, and said to Peter and the rest of the apostles, "Brethren, what shall we do?" And Peter said to them, "Repent, and be baptized every one of you in the name of Jesus Christ for the forgiveness of your sins; and you shall receive the gift of the Holy Spirit" (Acts 2:37-38).

Three thousand people were baptized on that day. In a few days the new converts numbered five thousand. The story of the mission of the apostles in those early days may be summed up in the words, "And the Lord added to their number day by day those who were being saved" (Acts 2:47).

The two instruments given missionaries are the Gospel and the Holy Spirit. The Christian message comes as a surprise to the world. The center of the message is Christ, and he is the initiator of faith and the bestower of salvation. In other religions it is man who seeks, hoping by his efforts to turn the gods' attention to him and give him what he seeks. Here it is Christ who seeks and finds man, not because man is deserving of God's attention but because of his grace.

Present at the gathering on the Day of Pentecost were "Parthians and Medes and Elamites and residents of Mesopotamia, Judea and Cappadocia, Pontus and Asia, Phrygia and Pamphylia, Egypt and the parts of Libya belonging to Cyrene and visitors from Rome, both Jews and proselytes, Cretans and Arabians" (Acts 2:9-11). They all heard them telling of Christ in their own tongues. (It seems strange that "Judea" is mentioned with other nations and nationalities, as it would be natural for Judeans to be in the capital of their country, Jerusalem, and to understand other Jews speaking to them. Because of the similarity between the Greek words for "Judea" and "India," the startling suggestion has been made by some exegetes that "India" should be read here instead of "Judea.")

These were among those who came to faith and were baptized to form the early Christian community. Philip preached to an

Ethiopian minister of Candace, the queen of the Ethiopians, and baptized him as he was on his way back to his home country. He also made an extended missionary journey to Samaria, and, when it proved successful, Peter and John were sent there. They too preached to the Samaritans, reaching many villages with the Gospel.[2] This early ministry to non-Jews would be an indication that the disciples of Christ of Jewish origin were willing to admit that Gentiles also had a part in the kingdom of Christ. Any hesitation Peter may have had about accepting Gentiles into Christian fellowship had certainly been removed before he baptized Cornelius, the Roman centurion. During his conversation with the centurion he said, "Truly I perceive that God shows no partiality, but in every nation any one who fears him and does what is right is acceptable to him" (Acts 10:34-35). It was Peter and James who defended Paul's practice of not requiring Gentile Christians to follow Jewish ceremonial practices. Paul was clear on this point, for he was convinced that he was called to be "apostle to the Gentiles." He wrote in his epistles concerning the relationship of Jew and Gentile within the Christian fellowship.

> Or is God the God of Jews only? Is he not the God of Gentiles also? Yes, of Gentiles also, since God is one; and he will justify the circumcised on the ground of their faith and the uncircumcised through their faith (Rom. 3:29-30).

> For there is no distinction between Jew and Greek; the same Lord is Lord of all and bestows his riches upon all who call upon him. For everyone who calls upon the name of the Lord will be saved (Rom. 10:12-13).

> One God and Father of us all, who is above all and through all and in all (Eph. 4:6).

> Therefore God has highly exalted him [Jesus] and bestowed on him the name which is above every name, that at the name of Jesus every knee should bow, in heaven and on earth and under the earth, and every tongue confess that Jesus Christ is Lord, to the glory of God the Father (Phil. 2:9-11).

There was seeming unanimity in the early church on the principle that the message of Christ is intended for all and therefore must be preached to all. Exegetes agree that this was the view of Paul, but, since Baur and the "Tübingen School," most writers on the early church have claimed that Paul differed from the other church leaders of the time in holding this view and that it resulted in a long-lasting bitter strife. This theory forced exegetes to do strange things in their interpretation of the Book of Acts. They felt Luke tried to cover up this difference in his report of the Jerusalem Conference in Acts 15. Paul did not approve of Peter's manner of fellowship with the Gentiles on one occasion, but there is no evidence of any basic difference in the fundamental issues of salvation and the Christian life. Peter and Paul were friends. Both presented the Gospel to both Jews and Gentiles. Paul went first to the Jewish people, but when they hardened their hearts against the message, he went to the Gentiles. There were, no doubt, differences of opinion between Paul and others, but he enjoyed fellowship with the leaders of the church in Jerusalem.

The "Tübingen School" held that Paul believed in the universalism of the Gospel while the other apostles and Christians believed in the particularism of the Gospel, that is, that it was for the Jews.

> In our time the sharpest criticism of Baur's view comes from Sundkler, who says rightly: "The opposition between particularism and universalism is the product of a modern cosmopolitan outlook, and has nothing to do with the biblical conception of the mission." One may add, as I did in "Israel and the Gentiles in the New Testament," that the very opposite of Baur's view is right. The primitive Church and Paul were universalistic as Jesus was, because they knew that the Gospel was for Gentiles as well as Jews, whereas the later Catholic Church lost that universalism.[3]

Present-day students of Paul and the early church have discarded what Munck calls "the heavy burden" laid upon them by Tübingen. It need no longer be questioned that the members of the early church were united in the conviction that the Gospel is for all men.

The twelve apostles had their call for the task of witness directly from Christ. Paul claimed his call too was directly from Christ, through special revelation, after the death of Christ. In speaking of his call, he not only mentioned his meeting with Christ on the Damascus road, but spoke of it in the same terms used by the Old Testament prophets. To the Galatians he wrote, "But when he who had set me apart before I was born [literally "from my mother's womb"] and had called me through his grace, was pleased to reveal his Son to me, in order that I might preach him among the Gentiles,

I did not confer with flesh and blood . . . " (Gal. 1:15). Compare
this with Jeremiah's call, "Before I formed you in the womb, I knew
you, and before you were born I consecrated you; I appointed you
a prophet to the nations," and also with Isaiah's call, "And now
the Lord says, who formed me from the womb to be his servant"
(Is. 49:5).

> When Paul applies these biblical expressions to his own call, he
> must be thinking, not only that he thereby illustrates God's call
> to him personally, but that that call is the same as it was in the
> case of Jeremiah and Deutero-Isaiah, a renewal of God's will
> for the salvation of the Gentiles, giving him a place in the his-
> tory of salvation in line with those Old Testament figures.[4]

There was a compulsion laid upon Paul, evident from the time
of the experience on the Damascus road, that reminds us of Jeremiah and Amos. Jeremiah did not seek the office of prophet, but
cried out to God in the midst of his life of witness, "Thou art stronger
than I, and thou hast prevailed" (Jer. 20:7). Paul wrote to the
Corinthians, "For if I preach the gospel, that gives me no ground
for boasting. For necessity is laid upon me. Woe to me if I do not
preach the gospel!" (1 Cor. 9:16). To proclaim the gospel was not
his own decision. His position was much like that of the prophet
Amos who declared, "The Lord took me from following the flock,
and the Lord said to me, 'Go, prophesy to my people Israel' " (Amos
7:15), and again, "The Lord has spoken; who can but prophesy?"
(Amos 3:8).

Paul wished to make clear to the people that he was not proclaiming his own or other men's wisdom, but that his message was from
God. There was authority in his preaching. The charismatic nature
of the message of the prophets was similar to the preaching of
God's Word in New Testament times. There was no set cult or
pattern, but the message was from God to the people.

The call may be less dramatic in our present day, but every true
missionary who goes out in the name of Christ has the assurance
of God's call and the conviction that the message of God is living
and vital for the people to whom he is sent.

Those who had been specially called and set aside for the proclamation of the Gospel were not alone in the work of proclamation. A
profound impact upon the world was made through effective witness of many Christians who continued to be active in business and

professional life. The rapid growth of the church in that early period cannot be ascribed only to the work of the apostles. Laymen were also under the burden of witnessing to Christ. The Hellenistic Jews who became Christians were among the first to spread the Gospel in Judea, Galilee, and Samaria. During the persecution which caused the dispersion of the Christians, they brought the message of Christ with them to the places where they settled. New churches were established in places not previously visited by those called to be preachers. There was a spontaneous growth of the church through the witness of its members. Some converts later became aids of the Apostle Paul.

The extent of the expansion of Christianity in the first century is amazing. The detailed record of the work of Paul is given in the Book of Acts. The other apostles were also busy. Early traditions give a marvelous record of their work. It is certain that Paul reached Palestine, Asia Minor, parts of Greece and Italy, and his Letter to the Romans indicates that he also made a missionary journey to Spain.

James the Elder witnessed in Jerusalem and was murdered there.

Peter served in Jerusalem, Judea, Galilee, and Rome.

John began his work in Jerusalem and was for a long time the pastor at Ephesus, where he had his base for reaching surrounding areas.

Andrew served in the Byzantine Empire, Thrace, Macedonia, and Greece.

Bartholomew, who possibly reached India, was a missionary in Armenia where he was later killed.

Thomas reached Odessa, Persia, and India. The "Thomas Christians" feel certain that he was the founder of their church along the Malabar Coast.

Matthew is said to have lived in Judea, Macedonia, and Ethiopia.

James, the son of Alphaeus, labored in Spain.

Judas Thaddaeus witnessed in Judea, Galilee, Arabia, Syria, and Mesopotamia.

Simon the Zealot is reported to have served as missionary in North Africa, reaching as far as Morocco.

According to tradition the apostles reached people of every level of society including those in high government circles in Rome, cultured Greeks, and leading officials of other nations. Besides the

Twelve, Timothy, Silas, Titus, Apollos, Barnabas, John Mark, Aquila, and Priscilla, mentioned in Paul's letters and in Acts, and a host of others of whom we have no record, spent their lives in the witness of Christ.

There were some sectarian developments in the early church that resulted from overemphasis on certain phases of Christian teaching to the neglect of others, and from an attempt to introduce Jewish practices into the Christian doctrine. There were also some false prophets who led people astray. In spite of external opposition and these internal problems, the church retained its basic unity of faith and practice and was spread to many lands in a very short period of time.

In their confession of faith early Christians placed a strong emphasis on the resurrection of Jesus Christ. Christians meeting each other would give the greeting, "Christ is risen," and receive the reply, "He is risen indeed." Accompanying this strong statement of faith was the belief in Christ's imminent return. Paul spoke frequently of the return of Christ, and mentioned this expected return in his letters to the churches.

Luke's account of Christ giving the "Great Commission" to the disciples was followed immediately by his report of the ascension.

> And when he had said this, as they were looking on, he was lifted up, and a cloud took him out of their sight. And while they were gazing into heaven as he went, behold, two men stood by them in white robes, and said, "Men of Galilee, why do you stand looking into heaven? This Jesus, who was taken up from you into heaven, will come in the same way as you saw him go into heaven" (Acts 1:9-11).

The apocalyptic utterances of Jesus stressed the need for watchfulness. "Watch therefore, for you do not know on what day your Lord is coming." In the early church there were places where there seemed to be a special emphasis on Christ's return, even to the point where men ceased to work and assembled to be ready to meet him. Paul wrote that there were certain things that would happen before Christ's coming, and urged them to live in the joy of faith in the present life.[5] The faith in Christ's imminent return was retained. The feeling of responsibility toward people without the knowledge of the Savior was the basic driving force of witness, but the thought of his return gave greater urgency to the message. The messianic promises of the Old Testament came into new focus, and it was the task of the Christians to bring all people into the fellowship of Christ, the true Messiah.

Paul himself was a convert from Judaism to Christianity. He who once persecuted the Christians became "the apostle to the Gentiles."[6] From the time of his conversion he was conscious of his missionary call. After a brief time of study in solitude he witnessed of Christ, but little is known of his work until Barnabas went to Tarsus, Paul's home town, to secure Paul's help in ministering to the young church in Antioch. The church there had been established by Christians from Phoenicia and Cyprus who had left Judea because of the persecution. Paul served as pastor with Barnabas in Antioch until his call as missionary to the Gentiles crystallized in a special way.

> Now in the church at Antioch there were prophets and teachers, Barnabas, Symeon who was called Niger, Lucius of Cyrene, Manaen a member of the court of Herod the Tetrarch, and Saul. While they were worshiping the Lord and fasting, the Holy Spirit said, "Set apart for me Barnabas and Saul for the work to which I have called them." Then after fasting and praying they laid their hands on them, and sent them off. So, being sent out by the Holy Spirit, they went down to Seleucia; and from there they sailed to Cyprus. When they arrived at Salamis, they proclaimed the word of God . . . (Acts 13:1-5).

This was the first of several missionary journeys Paul took into Asia Minor and Europe, preaching the Gospel and establishing congregations. The Book of Acts and the Epistles of Paul are the sources for rather extensive knowledge of the work carried out by him and his co-workers, and the principles and policies followed by them.

When Paul was selected by the church to go as missionary, the earlier, personal call to be missionary to the Gentiles was verified and implemented. This has been the pattern for sending missionaries since that time. Today, too, the church calls and sends men and women who have sensed the call of God to mission work. The church and the individual missionary share in the responsibility and in the work. The task of evangelizing the world is given of God to individual and to church. Some are to send. Others are to go.

The Scripture says, "No one who believes in him will be put to shame." For there is no distinction between Jew and Greek; the same Lord is Lord of all and bestows his riches upon all who call upon him. For, "every one who calls upon the name of the Lord will be saved." But how are men to call upon him in whom they have not believed? And how are they to believe in him of whom they have never heard? And how are they to hear without a preacher? And how can men preach unless they are sent? (Rom. 10:11-15).

The account in the Book of Acts concerning the calling and sending of Barnabas and Paul speaks of two sending agencies: "They [the church in Antioch] laid their hands on them and sent them off" and "So, being sent out by the Holy Spirit . . . " (Acts 13:3, 4). The importance of the act of the congregation in sending missionaries is emphasized, but that the church acts under the guidance of the Holy Spirit is of even greater significance. The church is the recognized agency through which the Spirit works.

Paul's missionary journeys were marked by the personal and public work that resulted in the formation of congregations in the cities he visited. There was essential unity among these throughout the Roman world. To Paul the church was intimately connected with the whole concept of the kingdom of God. The true church was called the "body of Christ" and the interdependence of the individual Christians as various members of the body and the interdependence of the congregations and smaller units of the whole were vital.[7] This church was brought into being by God through the Holy Spirit and therefore in union in Christ.

That is the constituent element of the Church. From this we are able to learn its nature, and thereby it can be concluded that in the deepest sense all organization is excluded. It exists or it does not exist. It cannot be organized, but grows from the Gospel that is preached.[8]

Man could simply attempt to bring those who received this newly-given life into contact with other believers so they would be able to keep, and grow in, the godly life worthy of Christians so that the whole church might be effective in witness. Believing in this inner spiritual unity among all believers with God as the author and perfecter of faith, Paul dared to trust in the continued work of the Spirit in the congregations. Freedom was given. The Christians elected their own leaders and were immediately left with the responsibility of retaining the faith and proclaiming it in the area where they lived. It was not Paul's purpose to live with a new congregation and form it according to his own pattern, but he left it, under God, and traveled on to evangelize other areas and start other congregations.

1. Paul went to areas where the Gospel had not previously been proclaimed. He did not wish to build on another man's foundation. He did not wish to duplicate efforts. The time was short, and his duty was to preach to all that could be reached in the time God gave him.

2. Paul went to political centers that were also centers of communication and transportation for larger areas. These were the cities of greatest missionary activity. The influence of witnessing members of the congregations in such cities could and would be spread to the entire area.

3. Indigenous churches were formed wherever Paul labored. Toward the close of his ministry, in each place, elders were elected to serve the Christians and be responsible for the missionary effort of that community. No aid was given for salaries, for erecting churches, or for extension of the Gospel. Many congregations first met in homes of the Christians, erecting churches as the number of believers warranted it.

4. The congregations had the responsibility of calling and sending men into missionary service and determining the policy under which they worked. The action of the elders of Antioch in calling and sending Paul and Barnabas was the first example of this.

5. Paul maintained close contact with the congregations in order to advise and direct them as occasion demanded. His letters to the various churches are evidence of this. Timothy and Titus, his co-workers, were sent by Paul to visit churches and reside in certain areas to give guidance and help to the growing Christian community. Paul also revisited some congregations—some once, others several times.

6. Each congregation became a center for spreading the Gospel. There was never any thought that the world could be evangelized

only by Paul, the twelve apostles, and others who might be selected for full-time service as missionaries.

7. The Christians in one area were conscious of the needs of those in other localities. When there was famine among the Christians in Jerusalem, as brothers in the faith, other congregations contributed to their relief (Cf. 1 Cor. 16:1-4).

There was a fluidity in the church that helped make its missionary work effective. Jerusalem was first recognized as the important center of the church, and the supposition is that Peter was the first leader there. He was followed by James when Peter left to go on missionary journeys. As the church spread westward, Antioch became the center for the work, and the church at Ephesus played a strong role. Later Rome was the center of Christian activity. There were also strong centers in North Africa and Syria. There was no theological significance in any of the geographical centers of the church. Christ was the center—and remained the unchallenged head of the church. Earthly centers were not fixed. They were chosen as the particular times and specific situations required— that the church under Christ might prosper.

There was no set form established by Paul for the organization of a congregation, as far as can be determined by the New Testament. In his early missionary work he appeared first in the synagogues where he preached to the Jews and their Gentile proselytes and friends. The electing of elders would indicate that the organization pattern of the synagogue was followed to some extent for the Gentile congregations. In the pastoral letters mention is made of a bishop, deacons, and elders, who apparently formed the church council. The qualifications demanded for each were quite similar, and there was no clearcut division in duties. By the time these letters were written, there was another group serving in the church called "widows" whose duty it was to minister to the poor and sick. The bishop was likely the chairman of the deacons who, with the elders, were responsible for the preaching, teaching, and general rule over the church.[9] There was a very simple type of organization. The elected men were responsible for the welfare and harmony among the members as well as for the outreach to the community.

The principles of Paul's mission and his procedures in evangelism have been regarded by many as the pattern that should be followed in subsequent mission endeavor. Certainly the basic core of the theological principles should be maintained, and there are, no doubt, other aspects that should be retained and practiced. But Paul had a spirit of pliability in regard to external methods and organization that his followers should also show in adapting methods to the age and area served, so that the message can be grasped and the church may be indigenous.

CHAPTER SIX

POST-APOSTOLIC MISSION

Rapid expansion of the church continued. The records from this period following the Apostolic Age are not as consistently good as those telling of Paul and his ministry. Most of the available information about the work of the other apostles in the apostolic period and of mission work from A.D. 100 to 325 (when Christianity was made the state religion of Rome) is found in scattered writings and traditions. Some of the traditions can be trusted. Some, though inexact, give a general picture of the times. Others are entirely spurious.

Eusebius, writing about 200 years after the death of the last apostles, is considered fairly dependable.

> Along the side of him [Quadratus] there flourished at that time many other successors of the apostles, who, admirable disciples of those great men, reared the edifice on the foundations which they laid, continuing the work of preaching the gospel, and scattering abundantly over the whole earth the wholesome seed of the heavenly kingdom. For a very large number of His disciples, carried away by the fervent love of the truth which the divine word had revealed to them, fulfilled the command of the Savior to divide their goods among the poor. Then, taking leave of their country, they filled the office of evangelists, coveting eagerly to preach Christ, and to carry the glad tidings of God to those who had not yet heard the word of faith. And after laying the foundations of the faith in some remote and barbarous countries, establishing pastors among them, and confiding to them the care of those young settlements, without stopping longer, they hastened on to other nations, attended by the grace and virtue of God.[1]

These zealous disciples covered new areas in Europe, Asia, and Africa. This period was in many ways difficult, opposition in some areas leading to persecution. Rarely did the states offer protection from violence. It was not till Christianity became the state religion of Rome that people found it politically desirable or economically advantageous to become Christians. Greater numerical growth came during the rule of Constantine, but people then entered the church for reasons other than faith. This period, up to the time of Constantine, is of special interest because it shows the power of the Gospel when it is preached by men of faith, with no external inducement to accept.

Syria. Antioch was established as the center of Christianity by Paul. There was a rapid development in the church both in the city and the surrounding area. The extent of its influence can be seen from comments made by Emperor Trajan when he visited there in the year 115. Interested in idolatrous worship, he found few opportunities because of the decadence of idolatry in the city. He became perturbed and sought to do everything possible to restore its early status and recommended that the Christian leader Ignatius be sent to Rome to be devoured by wild beasts in the arena. Little information can be found concerning the period following this event, but James Orr records that the church at Antioch was a center of ecclesiastical influence of first rank in the middle of the third century. Important church councils convened there, an important theological school was erected, and later the magnificent "golden church" was built. Christianity had prospered and been a power in the area even before Constantine's favor was shown. Chrysostom records that before the year 400 the Christians were a majority in the city.

Asia Minor. Work was most likely started in Asia Minor by Christians who had been scattered because of persecution in Judea. Apollos and Paul spent considerable time there, and John served as pastor of Ephesus until he reached a ripe age. The growth of the church continued through several generations. Seven churches in Asia Minor are mentioned by John in the Book of Revelation: Ephesus, Smyrna, Pergamum, Thyatira, Sardis, Philadelphia, and Laodicea. There were also churches in Colossae, Miletus, and possibly in Troas. Archeologists have in recent years excavated several churches in the city of Ephesus. One of them was a double church built on the foundation of a pagan building 800 feet long. They have also unearthed a stone cross set upon a pedestal that once held the figure of the goddess Artemis. The inscription reads, "Demeas has removed the deceitful image of the demon Artemis and in its place put this sign which drives away the idols, to the praise of God and of the cross, the victorious, imperishable symbol of Christ."[2]

Advance of the Christian church into North Asia Minor was noted by Governor Pliny. He indicated that in the year 112 the number of Christians had increased to such an extent that there was a danger that pagan worship would die out. He failed in his attempt to force the people to renounce Christ. He stated that "the faith" had reached rural areas and had established firm centers in the major cities.

In the middle of the third century, Gregory, a pupil of Origen, became pastor of New Caesarea in North Asia Minor. It is said that when he arrived, he found only seventeen Christians in the town, and that when he died thirty years later there were only seventeen pagans. Gregory of Nyssa wrote of him:

> Crowds used to gather in the morning when he preached, questioned, and admonished, instructed and healed. In this way, and by the tokens of divine power which shone forth upon him, he attracted multitudes to the preaching of the Gospel. The mourner was comforted, the young man was taught sobriety, to the old fitting counsel was addressed. Slaves were admonished to be dutiful to their masters; those in authority to be kind to their inferiors. The poor were taught that virtue is the only wealth and the rich that they were but the stewards of their property and not its owner.[3]

Persia. The early history of Christianity in Persia is filled with interesting tradition, much of which cannot be accepted. According to one tradition Prince Abgar wrote a letter to Jesus requesting him to come to Syria to heal him of a disease, and the letter was answered by Thomas saying that someone would be sent later. Copies of both letters are to be found in the collection *The Ante-Nicene Fathers.* An account of the introduction of Christianity into the country is found in a collection called *Preaching of Thaddaeus at Edessa.*

> After the ascension of our Saviour, the Apostle Thomas, one of the twelve, sent one of the seventy-six disciples, Thaddaeus, to

the city of Edessa to heal Abgar and to preach the Gospel, according to the word of the Lord. Thaddaeus came to the house of Tobias, a Jewish prince, who is said to have been of the race of the Pacradouni. Tobias, having left Archam, did not abjure Judaism with the rest of his relatives, but followed its laws up to the moment when he believed in Christ. Soon the name of Thaddaeus spread through the whole town. Abgar, on learning of his arrival, said: "This is indeed he concerning whom Jesus wrote to me"; and immediately Abgar sent for the apostle. When Thaddaeus entered, a marvelous appearance presented itself to the eyes of Abgar in the countenance of the apostle; the king having risen from his throne, fell on his face to the earth, and prostrated himself before Thaddaeus. This spectacle greatly surprised all the princes who were present, for they were ignorant of the fact of the vision. "Art thou really," said Abgar to Thaddaeus, "art thou the disciple of the ever-blessed Jesus? Art thou he whom He promised to send to me, and canst thou heal my maladies?" "Yes," answered Thaddaeus, "if thou believest in Jesus Christ, the Son of God, the desire of thy heart shall be granted." "I have believed in Jesus," said Abgar, "I have believed in His Father; therefore I wished to go at the head of my troops to destroy the Jews who have crucified Jesus, had I not been prevented by reason of the power of the Romans."

Thenceforth Thaddaeus began to preach the Gospel to the king and his town; laying his hands upon Abgar, he cured him; he cured also a man with gout, Abdu, the prince of the town, much honored in the king's house. He also healed all the sick and infirm people in the town, and all believed in Jesus Christ. Abgar was baptized, and all the town with him, and the temples of the false gods were closed and all the statues of idols that were placed on the altars and columns were hidden by being covered with reeds. Abgar did not compel any one to embrace the faith, yet from day to day the number of the believers multiplied.[4]

Kenneth Scott Latourette gives a brief historical summary, stating that Edessa might have been predominantly Christian by the beginning of the fourth century.

It was natural that the faith should soon win adherents in Edessa. Here was a city on the great trade routes which ran between the mountains of Armenia on the north and the Syrian desert on the south. Until the end of the second century it was outside the Roman Empire and within the sphere of influence of Parthia, one of Rome's most formidable rivals. On the border, it could expect attack from both sides, but for a time in the first centuries of our story it maintained an independent existence. . . . Not far from Antioch, that early center of missionary activity, it may be that Edessa received emissaries from the same church which sent out Paul and Barnabas. A tradition, indeed, traces the succession of the Bishops of Edessa to Serapion, Bishop of Antioch A.D. 190-203. Edessa was, moreover, an important center of Greek culture. . . . In Mesopotamia, too, were many Jews.[5]

It is entirely possible that Christianity entered at the time of Abgar, that it received royal favor, and made rapid headway. Traditions to that effect are too numerous to be ignored.

Syriac tradition is clear enough on the point, of course. According to this, Mar Adai (who is variously described as either the Apostle Thaddaeus or as one of the "seventy") came during the first century to Edessa and planted Christianity there. His disciple, Mari, starting from thence, became the true evangelist of Persia.[6]

There are sermons and epistles and shorter writings still extant, claiming the authorship of Thaddaeus. From them we learn that he served first as an evangelist, preaching much as the apostles had done, and healing. He also supervised the various churches. In Edessa a church was erected with the financial aid of the king. Assistance to the poor was given through the church, the king and the nobles granting aid for this purpose. The king and some nobles also participated in the preaching missions. Tradition affirms that a church was planted by Mar Maris in Seleucia-Ctisephon, the winter capital of the Persian kings before the end of the first century. Sacred writings were translated into the Syriac language in the second century. The first translation of the New Testament was into Syriac.

The Christians of Edessa were predominantly Syrian, but the earlier contacts were likely made among the Jews, as the Book of Acts mentions the "dwellers of Mesopotamia." By about the year 200 the Baalist symbols on the currency of the country were replaced with the cross. This was the first country to adopt Christianity as its official religion. After it became the state religion the number of Persians in the church increased. Missionary work also spread into border areas. "By A.D. 225 . . . more than twenty bishoprics are known to have existed in the Tigris-Euphrates Valley and on the borders of Persia."[7]

The lot of the Christian in Persia did not remain favorable indefinitely. Zoroastrianism replaced Christianity as the state religion. When Christianity was adopted as the religion of the Roman Empire, Constantine issued a plea for the safety of the Christians in Persia. The Christians were immediately considered adherents of Rome, the great enemy of Persia, so efforts were made to destroy them. The persecution broke out under Shapur, and reached its height in the year 343, continuing with various degrees of intensity for thirty-five years. The extent of Christian penetration of the country is noted by records that give the names of 16,000 pastors, monks, and nuns who were put to death. After a peace of forty years, another thirty-year period of persecution broke out. Though the number of Christians decreased, the church survived, and later became a part of the Nestorian Church in the Baghdad area.

Armenia. Armenia was the second state to adopt Christianity officially. The history of the church there was similar to that in Edessa. There is evidence that Christianity was introduced into Armenia previous to the year 300.

Gregory (the Illuminator) was the outstanding missionary. He was the son of a Parthian invader, the only member of his family not exterminated by the Armenians. He was rescued and taken to Asia Minor where he was brought up by a Christian. At the age of twenty-five he returned to Armenia and ingratiated himself with the king, Tiradetes III. When he refused to worship one of the idols of the king, however, he was tortured. It was then learned that he was the son of a former invader so he was thrown into a dungeon to die. He was kept alive for fourteen years by fellow Christians. Then King Tiradetes became sick, and his sister dreamed that the release of Gregory would produce healing. Tiradetes recovered, and granted Gregory freedom to preach the Gospel. Tiradetes and his family were converted, and a national council adopted Christianity as the state religion in the year 302. Gregory, ordained in Caesarea, returned with missionaries and in twenty days 190,000 people were baptized.

Gregory ordained six hundred men, trained for the ministry, who proclaimed the Word and established churches for a while with no opposition from the state. Persecutions broke out later, as they had in Persia, and here, too, there was an expanding, suffering church.

Egypt. Early contact of Egyptians with Christianity is certain.

In the large Jewish settlements in Egypt, Philo became a famed leader and successful director of a program of proselyting. "Dwellers in Egypt" who were present in Jerusalem on the Day of Pentecost may have brought the Gospel with them when they returned home. At least five writers, as early as the third century, stated that Mark labored in Egypt. Apollos, an evangelist in Ephesus before Paul's first visit to that city, was called an Alexandrian. Emperor Hadrian wrote a letter to Consul Servanus (117-138) protesting some actions of the Christians in Egypt so, by that time, they must have been numerous and strong enough to attract official attention. The early records are unsatisfactory and do not give a continuous story, but it is known that within one hundred years there was a thriving Christian community in Alexandria. There were twelve city parishes with pastors and church edifices. A noted catechetical school, established beside the great heathen university, served as a training school for both male and female missionaries. The first leader of the school was Pantaenus, well versed in Greek philosophy, who at one time took a missionary journey to India at the request of travelers who reported that missionaries were needed there. Clement succeeded him as leader of the school. He wrote a number of Christian books, among them *An Exhortation to the Heathen,* one of the earliest missionary books. Clement was driven out of Egypt in the year 202, and was succeeded by the noted church leader Origen. Celsus wrote a book attacking Christianity and Origen wrote in defense, refuting his arguments. This and other famous apologetic writings appeared during that era and were useful in missionary work.

As early as 235 a council was held in Egypt attended by twenty bishops. The evangelization of the country reached its culmination, perhaps, by the year 400 when Emperor Arcadius granted the Christians one of the heathen temples in Alexandria.

There were other strong Christian centers in North Africa, especially around Tunis and Algeria where there was outstanding leadership. Saint Augustine, bishop of Hippo, was the author of *City of God* and *Confessions.* There are said to have been over two hundred bishoprics and a theological seminary in North Africa. The strongholds of the church during the post-apostolic period were North Africa and Asia Minor.

Ethiopia. Christianity has a long history in Ethiopia. For hundreds of years the queens of the country were named Candace. One of the officers of the incumbent Queen Candace had been in Jerusalem for one of the Jewish festivals. He was likely either a Jew by birth or a convert to Judaism. On his way home he was reading the Book of Isaiah when Philip met him on the road between Jerusalem and Gaza. He was perplexed and asked about the meaning of the words he read. Philip told him of Jesus. He believed, was baptized, and "went on his way rejoicing" (Acts 8:39). It is probable that he brought the Gospel to Ethiopia and shared it with others. This may possibly have been the beginning of the ancient church in Ethiopia.

However, special mission work was conducted in Ethiopia about three hundred years later. A ship of traders stopped for water along the Ethiopian coast. Their ship was plundered, and all but two boys were killed. One of those boys, Frumentius, was hired as secretary to the emperor and remained to educate his sons. He was a Christian from Tyre and persuaded many of the Roman traders in Ethiopia to accept the faith. When finally released, he went to Alexandria and told Athanasius about the opportunities for witness in Ethiopia. He and others returned as missionaries in the year 338. The church established at that time has retained its identity and dominance in the country until this day, in spite of internal struggles and ecclesiastical manipulations by the early Roman Church.

India. According to tradition, Thomas the Apostle brought Christianity to India. There were Jewish colonists there. India was an important point along the trade routes of that day, and there were many people from the Near East coming and going, some of them establishing headquarters there for a time.

It is certain that Christianity was established there in the first century, but the first reliable record comes from the second, between the years 180 and 190. Pantaenus, head of the famous Christian training school in Alexandria, and teacher of both Clement and Origen, went on a trip to India.

> Jerome, in one of his letters, says, "Pantaenus was sent to India that he might preach Christ among the Brahmins." He found Christians already there and using an early edition of the Gospel of Matthew, from which he brought back a copy to Alexandria. There is no means of knowing the extent of the work of the primitive missionaries in India. At the Council of Nice (A.D. 325) there was present a "Bishop of India."[8]

The "Thomas Christians" of India, who are still a separate group that includes many well-to-do and influential people, seem to have existed without much difficulty within the caste-riddled society by forming a system of their own similar to the caste idea. They claim their origin is from Thomas and recent studies lend support to this claim. Indian leaders today accept, as proven fact, that Christianity was introduced in India very early.

> The time-honored tradition so dearly cherished by the Christians of Kerala is that St. Thomas landed at Malankara near Cranganur in A.D. 52, founded seven churches and established Christian communities in Keraland, converted, among others, several Nambudiri Brahmin families. . . . After he labored in Kerala, he journeyed across the southern peninsula to the Coramandel, or East Coast and was martyred and buried in A.D. 68 at Mylapore near Madras.[9]

This tradition, carefully tested with the *Acts of Thomas* (a record of the Apostle's work in India) and other historical records, seems plausible. However, most mission historians hold that the "Thomas Christians" date back to another Thomas who came during the Nestorian period.

The Christians of the post-apostolic period continued the work of witness much as the apostles and earlier Christians had done. The message was of the crucified and risen Christ. Contact was made first with the Jews in the region and spread from them to the native population as it had at the time of Paul. There were, however, some new developments in the organization of missionary activity.

1. There were men specially designated to carry on full-time work in evangelism. Some may have gone out under their own sense of "call" to this service, but most of them likely went with the knowledge and blessing of their church. Many gave their lives to this work.

2. There were some who traveled to the churches that had been established—teaching, counseling, and admonishing the Christians—much as Timothy and Titus, co-workers of Paul, had done. They are mentioned specially in the *Didache*.

3. There were prophets whose work was similar to that of the

Old Testament prophets. Mention is made of them in the Book of Acts in connection with Paul's ministry. This office was discontinued after some years.

4. Teachers were used throughout the period. Schools were an early feature of the Christian church. Some of them were for the children of the believers. Others were specialized training centers for pastors and missionaries.

5. Bishops were mentioned in the Pastoral Epistles, and the office was continued. At first a bishop was elected for each congregation. Later large areas with many congregations were under one bishop. One of the duties of the bishop, as leader of an individual congregation and as leader of a group of churches, was to lead and direct the work of winning the pagans to Christ. Mission work was at the center of the church program.

6. As in Armenia and Ethiopia, lay people were active. Extensive Christian work was begun in the area north of Armenia by a Christian woman who had been taken captive and became a slave of the queen. Her service and witness led the king to request missionaries from Emperor Constantine. The church among the Goths northwest of the Black Sea was also established by captives—Cappadocian Christians who persisted in their faith and witness of Christ among their captors.

7. Apologists came to the fore in this period. As Christianity spread throughout the civilized world, many opponents attacked it mercilessly with many different accusations. In order to defend the Christians, the apologists wrote books and pamphlets to show that the accusations were false and that Christ is the only Savior. These writings in defense of the faith also explained Christianity to non-Christian peoples. Many of them were of a distinct missionary nature. Some samples will illustrate the missionary concern of the writers and one method of approach to the non-Christians.

Tertullian, about the year 200, wrote, "The principal charge against the human race, the world's deepest guilt, the all-inclusive cause of judgment, is idolatry."[10] In the year 215 Clement of Alexandria wrote, in his letter to Diognetus, a defense of the Christian church and an attack on idolatry.

Look at the things that you proclaim and think of as gods. See with your outward eyes and with your mind what material they are made of and what form they happen to have. Is not one a stone, like the stones we walk on, and another bronze, no better than the utensils that have been forged for our use? Here is a wooden one, already rotting away, and one made of silver, that needs a watchman to protect it from being stolen. Yet another made of iron eaten by rust, and another of pottery, no more attractive than something provided for the most ignoble purpose. Were not all these things made out of perishable material? . . . They are all dumb, after all, and blind. They are without life or feeling or power of movement, all rotting away and decaying. These are the things you call gods, the things you serve. You Gentiles adore these things, and in the end you become like them. That is why you hate the Christians, because they do not believe that these objects are gods.[11]

The First Apology of Justine (dated 155), speaking of an incident that took place in Alexandria, is a little more positive.

So, then, we are called godless. We certainly confess that we are godless with reference to beings like these who are commonly thought of as gods, but not with reference to the most true God, the Father of righteousness and temperance and the other virtues, who is untouched by evil. Him, and the Son who came from him, and taught us these things, and the army of the other good angels who follow him and are made like him, and the prophetic Spirit we worship and adore, giving honor in reason and truth, and to everyone who wishes to learn transmitting (the truth) ungrudgingly as we have been taught.[12]

Much of the writing was positive teaching of the tenets of the Christian faith to show that Jesus Christ is the Son of God, the Savior of the world. The creeds of the church were used in instructing non-Christian people in the faith.

Political situations and internal differences in the church brought changes at the close of this era. When Christianity was accepted as the state religion in Rome, there was rapid development toward the north and the west. The westward direction taken by the church, and doctrinal differences, widened the breach between the churches of the East and the West, and they became more independent.

Another factor affecting the expansion of Christianity, especially in Africa and the Near East, was the Muslim advance that began in 632 at the time of Mohammed's death. By 697 Syria, Palestine, Caesarea, Egypt, Mesopotamia, Persia, and North Africa, as well as Arabia, had been conquered. Only sad remnants of the Christian churches were reminders of the solid Christian advance of the past.

In spite of the later failure of these Christian missions, what was accomplished by the men of vision of that early period was amazing.

> To one with imagination the amazing rapidity of the spread of Christianity must be apparent. The followers of Jesus began as a sect within Judaism. They succeeded in winning only a small minority of their fellow Jews. However, far from dying out or persisting only as a small cult, Christianity moved on into the stream of Hellenistic urban culture. In spite of the many cults and philosophies with which that world teemed, it quickly attracted a following, and by the end of the third century of its life, in many cities of the East, especially in Antioch, Alexandria, and those in Asia Minor, it embraced an important minority of the population and in a few places probably a majority. Nor did it remain exclusively at home in the Latin-speaking portions of the West, notably in the capital of the Empire and in North Africa. In the West, as in North Africa and Gaul, it had begun to gain adherents among those whose primary tongue was not Latin. In the East it was becoming naturalized in Armenia and among peoples who spoke Syriac. It had acquired a foothold among still other folk, including those of the older Egyptian stocks, some of the peoples of Arabia, probably of the Goths, and possibly the Georgians and the Indians.[13]

CHAPTER SEVEN

THE NESTORIAN MISSION

The massive impact of Christianity upon the West which began in the Roman Empire attained permanence through the uninterrupted efforts of individual members of the early Roman Catholic Church and by official actions of that church. A doctrinal and organizational unity, even though frequently of a political-ecclesiastical nature, helped to give stability and prestige to the church. Christianity became a part of the culture of the people in the West. This was not characteristic of the missionary efforts of the Eastern Church.

In the East, fluidity in the political life of nations, with shifting influences and loyalties, gave instability and uncertainty to all movements, including Christianity. No single nation or common culture developed there in which Christianity could establish its roots for expansion to other areas. There are, however, some outstanding examples of missionary expansion in the East during the early period of the church that are marked by vision and faith.

There was also a difference *within* the church that separated East from West. This was basically a doctrinal difference dealing with the nature of Christ and of the Holy Spirit. The Nestorians were condemned by the Council of Ephesus in 431 and after four years were driven into exile. The Persian Christians were not Nestorian at the beginning of their missionary activities, and there is a question as to whether the missionary training school at Edessa ever adopted Nestorian doctrines. Burkitt says that an analysis of Persian Christian writings shows that the doctrines of the church were not Arian.[1] Latourette agrees that the Persians were not won

71

over to Nestorianism until the fifth century. He gives some reasons for the change:

> The main steps were the removal to Mesopotamia of some of those exiled from the Roman domains because of their Nestorian views, the winning over by some of them to the school at Nisibis, the chief educational centre of the Mesopotamian-Persian Church, and the filling of many of the leading ecclesiastical posts with those trained at Nisibis and committed to Nestorian doctrines.[2]

There was another development as a result of doctrinal controversy and discussions. This development has been variously described in its relation to missionary activity. The Syrian view was simply that the Eastern Church undertook the spreading of the Gospel as its main objective while the Western Church was dissipating its energy in excessive concentration on doctrinal discussions. The East spread education together with its very intensive evangelistic program. Throughout Asia the term *Salabi* (from *Salab*, meaning "cross") was the title of a learned man. Bishops were found in Teheran, Ishpahan, Khorasan, Merv, and Herat in the fifth century. In the sixth century mission work was conducted in India and Ceylon. In the next succeeding centuries they were in Egypt, Cyprus, Afghanistan, Kurdistan, and Siberia.

Dr. Kraemer, dealing with the Western Church, gives the following analysis of conditions following Constantine:

> In this new stage of the Church's career, the development of rigid formulation began. Orthodoxy in the full sense of the word was born. In itself, a doctrinal formulation is, in the historical career of a religion, a wholesome and indispensable necessity, and we are accustomed to look from a great distance at these formative doctrinal controversies mainly under that angle. At that time, however, and also for future generations, that meant also something else and something more, and this "else" and "more" obtained prominence. That is to say, they functioned in fact as the creed of an ideology of a religious-social structure, which is a relative historical phenomenon, but which through the ideology was absolutized. One of the main consequences of this development was that the self-consciousness of Christianity became preeminently doctrinal, which is not in accordance with the hidden symphony of emphasis in the Biblical message.[3]

A different missionary effort developed in each of the two divisions of the church. To begin with, the concern over doctrine in the Western Church caused diminishing missionary activity. When interest in missions was revived, it became the movement of an organized body with prestige and power, relying on the support of state and cultural pressures as well as on the Word of God. It became clearly evident in its missionary program that the church was an *institution*. In the East, political and cultural powers were not centralized and the church could not advance as an institution under their support. Governments gave only occasional and fragmentary support to Christianity. The missionary effort continued to be the work of smaller groups and individuals who relied almost solely on the message of the Gospel as their means of advance. This is why the study of the Nestorian Mission is of special interest and profit.

Several conditions in the East favored the advance of Christianity at the beginning of missions among the Persians.

1. The religious cults of the East had been localized in an effort toward self-preservation in the face of the encroachment of Zoroastrianism and other religions. There had been attempts toward syncretism of religions, but these had failed. The local religions were weak and in some instances rejected by the people, so they gave little opposition to the Christian faith.

2. There was similarity between the cultures of the Persian missionaries and the people they served. Syrians understood Aramaic. The missionaries were Semitic. They did not have to learn a foreign language and customs before proclaiming the Gospel.

3. There was no Persian persecution of Christians for the first 300 years of the Christian era. The ruling classes sometimes aided in the Christianization of the people under their rule.

4. There was tension between the rulers of the East and Rome. The political leaders at times welcomed the missionaries as dissenters from Rome and felt that it might be to their political advantage to have them in their midst.

5. There were trade routes to the Far East that made travel comparatively easy and safe. The missionaries began their work along these arteries of communication, gradually spreading out from them into the country.

Edessa was the center for the early expansion of the Eastern Church. About the time that Constantine gave peace to the Roman Church, persecution broke out in Persia. War was declared between Persia and Rome, and in 350 Emperor Julian was defeated. Romans were forced to leave the country and many Christians were taken captive into the mountainous country where they continued to witness and where Christian centers sprang up. Because of the persecution, the center was moved from Edessa to Nisibis where a missionary school trained men for work in Persia and other countries. From the records we learn something of their training and method of evangelism.

> The course was three years. First year's course: The five books of Moses, the Epistles of Paul and the "Kodra" (a prayer book for every day of the year; Bible texts). Second year course: David's Psalms, hymns for the church service, and the rest of the "Kodra." Third year's course: The New Testament, explanatory commentary on the Bible, and the confessions of the Greek fathers, also with explanatory commentaries.[4]

The Nestorian Church built on foundations of the earlier churches that had been established in Persia, and advanced along the trade routes. Cloisters were built which became the centers for copying and distributing Christian literature. Over 2,000 titles, with 150 authors, are listed in the history of the Nestorian Church. All these writings were on parchment and many have been preserved. The cloisters were the centers for missionary work in the immediate area, and resting places along the route for missionaries proceeding to more distant lands. The Christian faith became rooted, and the cloisters, at the same time, served as a link between the Christian workers of most of the lands reached through the Nestorian ministry.

The missionaries themselves were poor, adapting themselves to the conditions of the people among whom they labored. They traveled on foot wearing sandals, a staff in their hands, and on their backs a basket filled with copies of the Scripture and other religious books. They received gifts—among them some large grants from the rulers of various tribes. They did not keep what they received, except what could be used directly for the extension of their work. They distributed the rest to those who were poorer. Some of the missionaries became martyrs for their faith, but they were followed by others who built churches and schools and extended the work into new regions.

The spread of Christianity under the Nestorians was phenomenal in many ways. By 672, when Baghdad was chosen as their center, the Nestorians had occupied the area which is now known as Iraq and Iran. They had many followers in Armenia, Mesopotamia, and Arabia. There were churches in Syria, Cyprus, and India, and they penetrated into China, Afghanistan, Turkestan, and Siberia. They had many centers in the vast area of Tartary. East of the Caspian Sea there were twenty-five metropolitan sees with a far greater number of bishoprics and numerous churches. Marco Polo reported from his journeys that trade routes from Baghdad to Peking were lined with Nestorian churches. The Muslim persecution of 699-815 did not greatly hamper the work of the Nestorians to begin with. By 1265 there were seventy bishoprics in twenty-five Asiatic provinces. This work was tolerated by the rulers at first, but was disrupted and finally destroyed by soldiers of the great Khans. In 1385 Tamerlane swept away every Christian institution and drove the remnant of the Nestorians into the mountains of Kurdistan. Their missionary work was severely hampered, but their zeal was not lost. Toward the end of the fifteenth century an embassy was sent to China, and there is information concerning their mission activity in four provinces as late as 1502. In the Near East remnants of the Nestorian Church continued to exist. Even today some are found in Iraq where they are like little insulated islands in the sea of Islam.

The Christian church in India is rich with early tradition of work by the Apostle Thomas. Part of this tradition is found in the *Acta Thomas*. After the ascension the apostles met in Jerusalem and divided the world into regions of mission responsibility. Thomas was assigned to India but refused to go, claiming physical inability. He declined even after having seen a vision of Christ tellng him to go. He was subsequently sold as a slave to an Indian king. Recognizing this as God's reply to his refusal, he went contritely and willingly. He witnessed of Christ in India by word and miracle and won a large following, including the king and many of his household. Arrested by a new king when he acknowledged that he recognized only Jesus as his master, he was killed by the thrust of four spearsmen, and is presented thus in Indian art. Before his death he ordained the king's son, Wizan, into the ministry.

This and other traditions concerning the beginning of the Christian church in India by St. Thomas have not been accepted by modern historians. This particular story was discredited because there was no trace found of a ruler named Gundaphar. Toward the close of the nineteenth century, however, excavations in the Punjab revealed that Gundaphar was a historical person, a king of Indo-Parthia who "lived and ruled in the middle of the first century, chronologically a contemporary of St. Thomas."[5] There were some Christians in India before the time of the Nestorians, but most historians consider the Christian witness of another Thomas to be the beginning of missions in India.

Native Hindu history of the Malabar Coast tells of a Nestorian who came and settled there as a merchant, and was followed later by two bishops who built a church. As there was considerable trade at that time between Persia and India this story is very plausible. Other similar records indicate that Christianity came through various people at the time of the Nestorian movement. The following account seems to be historically acceptable.

> In the middle of the fourth century with the visit of Thomas of Cana, we reach a new stage in the history of the Malabar Church. Thomas of Cana was a Syrian merchant. The story is that the Catholicos of Jerusalem hearing the needs of the Malabar Church sent Joseph, Bishop of Edessa, some priests and deacons and about four hundred people under the leadership of Thomas of Cana. They were well received by the local rajah and the people, and they settled in and around Maha-devapatnam, old Cranganore. This was about A.D. 345. The rajah seems to have given them a certain town, and bestowed upon them certain social privileges, inscribed on a copper plate. The fourth century was a period of persecution for Christians in Persia and a number of refugees might have come and colonized in Malabar.[6]

Travelers through India about that time reported finding Christians on both the east and the west coasts. Europeans who passed through India in the thirteenth and fourteenth centuries also found believers in Christ. Marco Polo wrote about Christians at the church of the Shrine of St. Thomas at Mailapur on the west coast and Quilon on the east coast. Jordan, a Dominican who lived a while in India in the fourteenth century reported many Christians scattered about in India, but said they were ignorant of their faith. Archeological evidence bears out these reports, as crosses, engraved plates, and other Christian artifacts dating from these periods have been found.

> One thousand years after the first Nestorian planting [of the church] in India the Portuguese found there one hundred villages composed entirely of Nestorian Christians, and in all the country 1,400 churches with 200,000 souls. These people paid a slight tribute to the Rajahs, but were governed in matters both temporal and spiritual by their own archbishop, who received ordination from the Nestorian patriarch in Persia. They used Syriac in all their church services, permitting their priests to marry and admitted no images in their simple meeting houses. Through native political oppression and through still more shameful Romish persecution they had been reduced at the time of Carey to 116 churches all told, 84 united to Rome and 32 still independent.[7]

The report that Syriac was used in the churches would cause us to doubt the extent of their mission work. They seem to have established a caste of their own wherever they went, and were thus to some degree separate from other people, all belonging to their particular castes, the lines of which could not be crossed. There is, however, still in existence a church that dates back to the Nestorians.

> To remind Malabar Christians of the twelve centuries of Babylonian connections, there is still a Nestorian church in and around Trichur. The members of the church claim to be the true inheritors of the bishops sent by the Babylonian Patriarch who is now in America. They are an exclusive community and do not encourage intermarriage with others. They are also called Chaldean Christians. They number about 10,000. Besides the very old cathedral church at Trichur, they have nine other churches. They have a bishop in India at present besides six priests and six deacons. The present Bishop Mar Thoma has been sent by the Nestorian patriarch in America. . . . The Church under the new bishop is striving to organize and expand its activity in different fields.[8]

Besides the Syrian Church there is the Mar Thomas Church, now separated from the other group. A late British census taken in

India reported 2,467 members of the church, most of them well-to-do, successful in business, and maintaining a good relationship with the government.

Dr. A. C. Moule reports that Nestorians were in China in A.D. 635 to 845 and from the 12th century to about 1360. The date accepted by most historians is 635, but it is possible that there had been earlier contact of Christianity with the people of the empire. Jerome wrote in the year 403 from the monastery at Bethlehem:

> From India, from Persia, from Ethiopia, we daily welcome monks in crowds. The Armenian bowman has laid aside his quiver. The Huns hear the Psalter, and the cold of Scythia glows with a warm faith.[9]

It is well established that two Nestorian monks carried silkworms from China in a hollow bamboo in the year 551 and presented them to Emperor Justinian so that silk culture might be begun outside China. There are definite accounts of mission efforts begun in 635. In 1625 a Nestorian monument was discovered at Sianfu. This monument is still in existence and is of great interest to students of early Christian endeavor in China. Part of the inscription on this monument reads (translated from the Chinese):

> When T'ai Tsung, the polished Emperor, was beginning his prosperous reign in glory and splendour, with light and wisdom ruling the people, there was in the land of Ta-ch'in one of high virtue called A-lo-pen who, auguring by the blue clouds, carried the true Scriptures; watching the harmony of the winds, hastened to meet difficulties and dangers. In the ninth Cheng-kuan year (635) he came to Ch'ang-an. The Emperor sent the Minister of State, Duke Fang Hsüan-ling, to take an escort to the west suburb to meet the guest and bring him to the palace. When the books had been translated in the library and the doctrine examined in his private apartments, [the Emperor] thoroughly understood their propriety and truth and specially ordered their preaching and transmission. In the twelfth Cheng-kuan year, in the Autumn in the seventh month, it was decreed saying: . . . If we carefully examine the meaning of the teaching it is mysterious, wonderful, full of repose. If we look at the fundamental principle it fixes the essentials of production and perfection. In its speech there is no multitude of words; in its principle there is [perfect accomplishment] forgetting the means. It is the salvation of living beings, it is the

wealth of men. It is right that it should have free course under
the sky. Let the local officers therefore build a Ta-ch'in monastery in the I-ning quarter at the capital with twenty-one men
as regular monks. When the virtue of the ancestral Chou
failed, the dark rider went up toward the west; now that the
way of the great T'ang shines, a brilliant breeze blows toward
the east.

The great Emperor Kao Tsung was well fitted to succeed his ancestors; he adorned and glorified the true principle. Therefore he
founded brilliant monasteries in every one of the departments
(*chou*). And further he promoted Alopen to be Great Spiritual
Lord, Protector of the Empire. The religion was spread over the
ten provinces and the kingdoms were enriched with vast prosperity; monasteries occupied every city and the families enjoyed brilliant happiness.

In the Sheng-li years (A.D. 699) the Buddhists audaciously
raised their voices in Eastern Chou; at the end of Hsien-t'ien
(A.D. 713) the vulgar gentry greatly mocked, blasphemed, and
slandered in Western Hao. There were however Lo-han, head of
the monks, and Chi-lieh of great virtue, both noble sons of the
Golden Quarter (the West), unworldly eminent monks. They
supported together the mystic cord and joined in tying the
broken knot.

The most religious Emperor Hsüan Tsung ordered the prince
of Ning-kuo and the four other princes to go in person to the
Temple of Happiness to build and set up the altars and courts.
The beam of the religion had been weak for a moment but
was raised again; the stone of the Way had been thrown down
for a time but stood upright once more. . . . Su Tsung, the
polished and enlightened Emperor, refounded the brilliant
monasteries in Ling-wu and four other departments. Boundless
goodness came to help and happy fortune began; great prosperity came down and the Imperial estate was established.[10]

The above account shows that the Nestorians were given imperial sanction as well as land for a monastery and assistance in
erecting their buildings. The toleration edict of the year 638 has
survived among the Imperial Rescripts of the T'ang Dynasty.
It reads:

In the seventh month of the twelfth year of Cheng-kuan he issued this proclamation: The way has no constant name, nor the
Sage a constant form. According to environment religion is set
forth quietly affording salvation to all the living. The Persian

monk Alopen, bringing a scriptural religion it is mysterious, wonderful, spontaneous producing perfection, establishing essentials, for the benefit of man. It ought to be spread throughout the Empire. The Officers of works is to build in the I-ning ward one monastery to house twenty-one monks.[11]

But the account also tells of some attacks. Being favored by government is not always a blessing, as fortunes are apt to change with each new dynasty. There were periods of growth and decline until 845. Up to that time the leaders of Nestorianism in China were perhaps foreign. At least many of the monks were foreign.

Under such circumstances it is not surprising that a single imperial edict accomplished its ruin. In 845 the Emperor Wu Tung, a devotee of Taoism, ordered Buddhist monks to return to private life and included Christians in his sweeping proscription. From this blow Christianity did not recover. Probably its decay was hastened by the domestic disorder which accompanied the decline of the T'ang Dynasty and by the growing insecurity to foreign life and property. In 877-878 we hear of Christians in one of the ports, but significantly, as perishing in the capture of the city by rebels. In 987 a monk, who with five colleagues, had been sent to China seven years before to put the Church in order, told an Arab in Baghdad that he had found no Christians in the realm.[12]

However, Roman Catholic missionaries, coming later, found Nestorians and had to compete with them for influence over the people in the land of the Mongols. Missionary Ricci wrote on July 16, 1605, that they came to know for certain that there had been a number of Christians in China for the past five hundred years. There were traces of the church still existing in the eighteenth century, but beyond that time there is no record. There has been much speculation as to the reason for the failure of the Nestorians and there are many implied indictments against them. No sure answer has been given. It must be remembered that the well-organized Catholic missions failed at about the same time. The following reasons for the Nestorian mission failure in China are among those given.

1. Persecution. The Chinese religions are not exclusive. A person may be Buddhist, Confucianist, and Taoist at the same time. It might be that Christianity, demanding undivided loyalty to the one God, aroused the opposition of the Chinese people. It is also

possible that the successes of the Nestorians aroused the enmity of the religions of the realm. There were, during the period of the Nestorians, some rather strong uprisings of Buddhism and Taoism that would be intolerant of any opposition. Persecution may have resulted, but most Christian churches, if firmly founded in the faith, have been able to survive persecution.

2. Diminished support from the sending church may have been a factor. With the losses of territory and peaceful existence in Persia it may have been impossible to send necessary support in manpower and funds to continue a missionary program.

3. Historians have questioned the degree to which the church was indigenous. Most investigators have indicated that they found little control or leadership of the church by Chinese Christians. This criticism may be justified, but there are many Chinese as well as Persian names carved into the Nestorian monument. The Syrians may, however, have been more prominent in the church and more influential in forming its policies.

4. Dependence on political favor may have contributed to their failure. Such favor may make possible rapid growth, as it did in Europe, and such growth may be maintained under stable governments, or under governments deeply influenced by a powerful church. Here, however, with policies changing at the whim of new emperors, political favor may have proved disastrous.

5. Syncretism may also have been a contributing factor. This theory has been advanced since the discovery of the Sian monument. The fact that the cross carved at the top of the monument is set in clouds and lotus flowers, suggests that there was an attempt at syncretism with Buddhism and possibly also with Taoism. If this were true, it would naturally affect the Christian nature of the faith and rob it of its power. However, the artist who carved the stone may simply have put the clouds and lotus flower in for decoration, or to show the cross rising *above* the religions of the land.

CHAPTER EIGHT

MISSION IN
THE MEDIEVAL PERIOD

Mission development in the West, following the post-apostolic period, contrasted in many ways with the expansion in the East. There was little cultural difference between the people of the Roman Empire and the missionaries, so the work could continue as it had been conducted. Only occasionally was there government opposition to Christianity, so the church was free to continue expanding its efforts. But a change *within* the church slowed the missionary advance. The teaching program of the church became centered in the established churches, and less emphasis was placed on extensive missionary work.

Constantine's edict of toleration in 313 ushered in a new era called the medieval period of missions. Christianity became the favored religion and was adopted as the state church of Rome. Constantine's act added prestige and power to the church.

> He showed this favor by summoning his vassals to renounce pagan superstition and embrace the belief in the true God. He omitted no means of overthrowing paganism, and at least drove it from the cities; forbade pagan cults (at least all the immoral ones) and sacrifices (at least secret sacrifices and those appointed for his officials); ordered the closing and destruction of many temples and the removal of many idols; to some extent proclaimed the Gospel personally, and by his own actions brought thousands of adherents into the Church; but above all, by the founding of a Christian dynasty he made permanent the Christian character of the Roman Empire and thus transformed it into a radiant center for missionary activity.[1]

Dr. Glover gives a different evaluation of the state support of the church and its effect on its missionary activity.

> Viewed from without this seemed a glorious triumph for the faith, and it is true that it meant new safety of profession and liberty to preach. But in reality it wrought grievous injury to the true cause of Christ through the influx into the Church of great numbers of persons who were Christian in name only. The foes which had previously threatened the Church from without now began to attack it from within. Purity of faith and simplicity of worship were gradually lost, and spiritual declension set in. Missionary zeal and activity at once began to wane.[2]

The period of medieval missions, generally considered to have begun at the time of Constantine, reached full development during the barbarian invasion of Rome, and extended to about the year 1300. The first years of this period were marked by the mission work of individuals, but later there were mass conversions by united pressure from the state and the Roman Church.

The situation changed radically with the barbarian invasion. The missionaries had to begin dealing with people of different culture, language, and educational standards. Many of the invaders were still on a tribal basis and an individual could not become a Christian unless he severed his relationship to the tribe or persuaded the tribe as a whole to adopt Christianity. A few barbarians had become Christians through the ministry of the Nestorians and manifested their faith in sparing women and children, and saving the churches, in the cities they captured. They were the exception, however, and the barbarians presented a new mission field.

> From this point on, vocational missionaries appeared . . . and superseded the general Christian community as the agent of conversion. Monastic asceticism and organization made these missionaries specially adapted for their task, and they were more strongly supported than they had been previously by the ecclesiastical hierarchy and by state aid.[3]

The broader goal of Christianizing whole peoples or groups of people had been the aim when individuals, under the church or connected with a monastery, bore the burden of mission work. It was stressed even more after state and church united in efforts to increase the power of the church and extend its geographical boundaries. The missionaries and the churches they established were, as a rule, connected with the ecclesiastical hierarchy of Rome.

The first great missionary among the Goths was Ulfilas (311-388). He was born in their territory, son of Christian captives. He retained his Christian faith, and when he was sent on to an embassy to Constantinople at the age of twenty, he remained there to study theology. After ten years he returned as missionary and led the entire people to the faith, reduced the language to writing, and translated most of the Bible for the young church.

Martin, bishop of Tours (316-396), the patron saint of France, adopted a method that proved successful and was followed by others later. With a group of monks, he went through the area destroying temples and idols and proclaiming the Gospel.

There were Christians in Great Britain as early as A.D. 200 but little is known of their history. There is evidence that there was an organized church with its own bishop by the year 300. In 431 Pope Celestine insisted on a mission to Ireland but it is not known whether work was started at that time. According to accepted history it was Patrick who brought Christianity to the Irish. Patrick (396-493) was of Scottish birth. He was taken captive by the Irish at the age of sixteen but escaped to France where he attended monastic schools and received a good education. On returning to his home, he felt convinced of a call to go to Ireland as a missionary. With other monks he went there, established monasteries, and in his lifetime saw the country Christianized.

Columba (521-606) was the missionary to Scotland and the islands of the Hebrides, Orkney, and Shetland. Of royal birth and good education, he had founded several monastic communities in Ireland and then became interested in missions among the Scots. With twelve men he reached Scotland in 563. On Iona, an island which was the center of Druid superstitions, they established a Christian center which trained many monks who later became missionaries to the mainland of Europe. Scotland was Christianized by Columba and his co-workers.

After the early Christian era in England, the country had been invaded by the Anglo-Saxons who had destroyed the churches. Some of the Christian Celts retained their faith, but it was only in the far north and west that the Celtic church could continue to function. There they isolated themselves against the invaders whom they hated, and no attempt was made to Christianize them.

Pope Gregory the Great desired to Christianize England, and in the year 596 he sent Augustine and a company of monks there from Rome. After some hesitation and delay, they arrived and presented themselves to king Ethelbert, whose wife was a Christian. They were well received. Ethelbert was baptized. Within the year parliament adopted the faith and in a single day 10,000 people were baptized. This was the first official missionary group sent by the Roman Church and a close bond was established between Rome and England. Among letters sent by Pope Gregory to the missionaries was the one containing his "rule and code of Christian missions." In that, evidently in response to questions received from England, he said that pagan temples were not to be destroyed, but that the idols should be destroyed, and the temples converted into Christian places of meeting. The kingdom was soon secured for Christianity. Under instruction from Pope Gregory, two metropolitans were established, one at Canterbury and one at York, with twelve bishops under each.

Boniface (680-755) has been considered the greatest missionary of central Europe and a man who had deeper influence on the history of Europe than any other Englishman. It is also said of him that he "takes a prominent place in the Medieval Mission, which in many respects is similar to that of Paul in antiquity, or Francis Xavier in modern times."[4] He was of noble birth and was educated in an English monastery where he remained till he was forty years old. Moved by the tales of suffering of Willibrord in Frisia (Holland), he decided to go there to work with him. He had a very successful ministry in central Europe, and his work illustrates the new trend in European missions. The work there, up to this time, had been conducted semi-independently from Rome. After working a while in Frisia he was called to Rome (722) and was consecrated as bishop of the German frontier, through an oath of direct allegiance to the Pope. Armed with letters of protection to the rulers and of commendation to all Christians and influential people, his future activity initiated a new missionary phase. The expansion of Christianity now was through connection with Rome and the expanding Roman Church.

With this trend in missions came the centralized power and authority of Rome over the countries to whom missionaries were sent. In the year 800, Pope Leo crowned Charlemagne as emperor. This binding of military and Christian expansion together, under the name "Holy Roman Empire," continued for over a thousand years. Individual missionary work that was done was often given support by the state, and in that way was brought into the same orbit as the church-state-sponsored missions. Charlemagne's activity set a pattern.

> It was under Charlemagne that the systematic conversion of the Saxons began, and the mission was closely associated with his military and political action. It is characteristic of the king that, during his very first campaign (772), he destroyed not only the military center of Eresburg, but also the national religious shrine of Irminsul, and distributed their treasures among his retainers. . . . It was . . . after the suppression of the third rebellion (776) that the Saxons, as a guarantee of their sincere change of mind, bound themselves by oath to receive baptism and to preserve their Christianity faithfully under pain of confiscation of their property. . . . But the inflexible people revolted again under Wittekind or Widukind (782): once more the missionaries were expelled or murdered, the churches destroyed and the Christian Saxons compelled to apostatize. Then followed the massacre of Verden: while the execution of 4500 Saxon nobles may have some legal justification, it was a ghastly deed for which we can see no warrant. . . . On Christmas Day 785, the Saxon leaders, Wittekind of Westphalia and Albion of Eastphalia, accepted baptism at Attigny. Charlemagne was thus able to report to Rome the conversion of the whole Saxon people and order the celebration of a universal Christian feast of thanksgiving.[5]

The Scandinavians were later converts to the church, and by 1386 all Europe was considered officially Christian.

From the record so far we have some indication of the missionizing methods used. The advance, strongly connected with force, was followed with instruction in the Christian faith by monks and catechists. There was an effort to bring true understanding and Christian faith to the hearts of the people who had formally accepted Christianity. The preaching—like that of the apostles and missionaries of the post-apostolic period—was plain and direct, telling of Christ as the Son of God, God as Creator and Lord. With the message, there were frequent attacks on paganism. From Joceline's book, *Kentigern's Life,* we have an example of the sixth century approach to the Celts.

[Kentigern] showed that idols were dumb, the vain inventions of man, fitter for the fire than for worship. He showed that the elements in which they believed as deities were creatures and formations adapted by disposition of their maker to the use, help and assistance of men. But Woden, whom they, and especially the Angles, believed to be the chief deity . . . and to whom the fourth day of the week is dedicated, he asserted with probability to have been a mortal man, King of the Saxons, by faith a pagan, from whom they and many nations have their descent. His body, he continued, after many years had passed, was turned into dust, and his soul, buried in hell, endureth the eternal fire. By these and similar arguments casting forth the worship of idols from their hearts he proved to them the Almighty God . . . . [6]

A graphic example of this type of approach is found in the mission of Boniface.

On one occasion, finding that many of his converts had returned to their old Thor worship, he seized an ax and in the presence of thousands of enraged heathen and trembling half-Christians cut down a sacred oak of Thor. When the mighty tree crashed to the ground and Boniface was not, as they expected, stricken by a bolt from heaven, the people shouted his praise and came in thousands to be baptized.[7]

After this manifestation of the pagan god's weakness, there was a presentation of the Christian doctrine of God, the Trinity, and salvation through Christ, with emphasis on the promise of God's blessing on his followers, both in this life and the life to come.

Later in this era the message of Christ was supplemented with promise of the power and prosperity of Christendom as identified with the Roman civilization and the Christian church. The church, sustained by rulers in the Christianized areas, granted great political and economic benefits to those who became Christian. There were also warnings, on the other hand, of dire reprisals from kings and God on those who did not yield to the demands of the Christian emperor and his emissary, the missionary.

Emphasis was placed on the use of the baptismal sacrament. Baptism was often administered under force of arms, or with the permission of officials on behalf of the people—performed frequently with no preliminary instruction or evangelizing. Otto of Bamberg, missionary in Pomerania, did little preaching. When he approached a community he asked if they were ready to be baptized. If they were willing, he gave brief instructions and baptized them immediately. It was only when they declined that he became a persuasive preacher.

The monasteries were a powerful missionary force in most lands. They were the educational center for the people, the training center for monks and missionaries, and the example of what Christianity should be. In many places land grants were received from the nobility. These were turned by the monks into farms for supporting their work, and for instructing the people in farming methods.

An outstanding characteristic of medieval missions was the prominent part played by rulers in the conversion of their people. It was generally accepted that the chief or ruler should determine the religion of his subjects.

Addison lists several ways in which this principle was manifested:

> The three main types of which our period offers instances are: 1) independent rulers, recently converted and free from external pressure, exerting influence over their own countrymen; 2) monarchs of Christian lands extending their protection to missionaries among the weaker or dependent neighboring peoples; and 3) Christian conquerors exercising force against alien non-Christian races. England and Scandinavia supply us with the best examples of the first type; the Frankish rulers aiding Willibrord and Boniface are of the second type; and the third can be illustrated by the campaigns of Charlemagne against the Saxons and Teutonic Knights in East Prussia.[8]

In most instances, the missionaries first sought to secure the approval of the ruler of an area where they started work. When he gave them his support he frequently sent his own emissary with the missionaries to give them prestige when they went on their evangelistic trips. These emissaries were sometimes empowered to issue orders to the people to become Christian and to voice threats if they didn't. Many missionaries were dependent upon the financial support of the ruler where they were serving.

This relationship between missionary effort and civil authority had many effects. Rapid mass conversion rather than painstaking conversion of individuals resulted where the ruler gave support. Some missions were abandoned because of lack of such support. In a shift of rulers—through death or conquest—the fortunes of the church established by the missionaries was almost as precarious as that of the individual ruler who had given his support. On the other hand, it was true that where a mission was permitted to carry on its activities (even under intimidating methods) for any length of time, a solid church was established. It was later strengthened by missionaries who came to instruct, conduct services, and complete the organization in connection with Rome.

Many illustrations can be given to show the three ways in which missions were influenced by rulers during this period. King Ethelbert and King Edward of England not only gave missionaries permission to carry out their work, but often joined them to add their influence and authority.

Norway possibly gives the most outstanding example of a ruler exerting influence to convert his own countrymen—though the methods used might not be approved. Olaf Tryggvesson was born about 964. Much of his youth was spent on Viking cruises, raiding the coasts of Scotland, Ireland, and England. On one of these raids he was baptized. Some years later he was confirmed by a bishop in England. The following year he returned to Norway, was given a warm welcome by the people, and became king of the country. As king, he declared he would convert all Norway to Christianity or die in the attempt. He first gathered together his own relatives, who were leaders among the people, and persuaded them to be baptized and have all the people under them baptized. He then called an official assembly of the people in every section of Norway, and placed before them the choice of Christ or their pagan worship. To begin with, the choice was "democratic" or free, but when he met opposition he did not hesitate to use force, surrounding the people with his own army and killing those who opposed him. The people knew that the actual decision they had to make was whether to be baptized or be killed. It did not take long for Norway to become formally Christianized!

> The mass baptisms . . . and the destruction of idols and temples may have had little effect on the lives of the people still pagan in substance, but they lowered the prestige of the ancient religion and loosened the bonds which attached men to their gods. The very fact that the folk of Norway were nominally Christian and, in form at least, had accepted the new faith gave their king a right to undertake that process of organization and enforcement which was his main achievement. The further facts that

there was no regular pagan priesthood and that no deliberate reaction had since taken place made progress the less difficult.[9]

It remained for the following king, Olaf Haraldsson, to confirm the acts of Tryggvesson by uniting the people in their new faith, and by 1021 there were few places left in Norway where Christianity had not been accepted.

Charles Martel was a monarch of a Christian land who aided missionaries in their work among non-Christian people. Under his protection, Boniface had access to unevangelized areas. Through the influence of Charles, Boniface was also able to carry on a work which was of military as well as spiritual advantage. Boniface wrote to Bishop Daniel of Winchester in 746:

> Without the protection of the King of the Franks, I can neither rule the people of the Church nor defend the priests and clergy, the monks and the nuns of God; nor can I avail to check even the heathen rites and the worship of idols in Germany without his mandate, and the fear of him.[10]

Charlemagne was one of the Christian political leaders who united the aims of conquest and Christianization by use of the sword against alien, non-Christian races.

> But King Charles, always devoted to the Lord (for he was a most Christian man), began to consider how he might win this people to Christ. After he had listened to the counsel of the servants of God, he asked them to prevail upon the Lord through their prayers that He might look with favor upon his desires. Then, after he had brought together a great army and had invoked the name of Christ, he set out for Saxony. He took with him a throng of clergy—abbots and priests—all orthodox defenders of the faith, that they might cause the people (who from the beginning of the world had lain bound in the chains of the Evil Spirit) to take upon them, as believers, the mild and gentle yoke of Christ. When the king came thither he converted the greater part of that people to the faith of Christ, partly by the sword, partly by persuasion, and partly through gifts. Not long after he divided every province into episcopal districts and gave to the servants of the Lord power to teach and to baptize.[11]

This type of missionary conquest had its effect on the relationship between the converts and the missionaries. The missionaries were the conquerors who had to sustain control over the area by the same token of force used to win it. They also established a type of paternalism over the people which, though ecclesiastical, was like that of an overlord over subject peoples. The law demanding payment of a tithe to the church was strictly enforced, and only on certain occasions, through political manipulations, was the burden of the tithe eased. The people naturally looked upon such a tithe as an enforced payment to the conqueror rather than as a gift to the cause of Christ through the church. The few men within the church who spoke against enforcing payment of the tithe on the newly Christianized people did not prevail.

There were many aspects of missionary development during this period that committed ecclesiastical results to the precarious balance of secular power. We can only marvel that through these methods— or in spite of them—anything of permanent character and blessing could result. A survey of this brevity cannot bring out all the facets of the mission work in this period of struggle and strife. Though many of the methods used would be condemned as unspiritual (to say the least), there *was* honest zeal, strong faith, and earnest effort. Though many mistakes were made, the final result was a Christian Europe.

CHAPTER NINE

EARLY CATHOLIC MISSIONS

In the victorious forward march of Christianity, the Catholic mission fills a vital place. . . . No one should overlook it, as it is in greatness and expanse on a par with the Protestant, and in age and unity far ahead of it.[1]

If we examine the mission activity of the Catholic Church in the sixteenth, seventeenth, and eighteenth centuries, we will witness a truly glorious picture. This picture is not only one of outward significance, in that there was some true spiritual power there. It is the deepest root of Christianity in the Roman Church that satisfies its longing in this way to serve the Lord in the greatest cause of his kingdom. That is why Catholic mission history affords us so many glorious examples of courageous faith and endurance unto martyrdom.[2]

Intense missionary zeal within the Catholic Church was exemplified in some of the mission leaders of the Middle Ages. Their zeal was not universal within the church, but they did much to arouse a church-wide consciousness of missions and to establish responsibility for mission progress and method upon the church officials. Through the individual missionaries and mission orders we also have patterns of mission methods and policies so varied in nature that "Catholic Missions" cannot be classified under any one of them. In some places there was accommodation to social and religious concepts of people among whom the Catholic missionaries worked to a point where syncretism resulted. In other places there was a thorough transplanting of the *Roman* Church to foreign soils. Many stages in approach between the two extremes were tried, providing a rich field for study of mission method.

92

One of the main differences between Catholic and Protestant missions is in the attitude toward the church. According to Catholics, salvation is to be found only within the Roman Church, so her aim has been the expansion of the authority of the church over the mission fields. Hendrik Kraemer speaks of the emphasis of the Roman Church as being less on the proclamation of a message than on the maintenance of the church as a hierarchical institution and keeper of the infallible truth.[3] The presence of the church is itself a witness. This may be considered a *broader* witness than that emphasized by the Protestants, as confidence is placed in the gradual influence of the church, as an institution, upon society. The impact of the church on society is often considered of more immediate importance than the winning of an individual.

> For this reason the requirement of knowledge and moral excellence as prerequisites to baptism is more flexible in Catholic missionary practice. The immediate aim is less to make individually strong Christians than to lead peoples as a whole into Christian conceptions. Such a procedure is likely to result in many relatively uninformed and immature believers, as the Constantinian age illustrated, and Catholic missionaries are frank to admit this fact. Yet their desire to make loyal Catholics first, then mature Christians, is quite consistent with modern Catholic missiology.[4]

The Protestant emphasis is less on the existing church as an hierarchy than on the church to be built by individuals with faith kindled by the message of redemptive power. The church is considered as the agent to bring the message, but on the mission field the church is the result of the message that has been proclaimed. It is in the Word that there is union between the sending and receiving churches, and this is the reason for the stress Protestants put on the use of Scriptures as basic, above all else, in the mission program.

There was a lull in missionary activity during the Middle Ages, which extended into the period of the Reformation. Scholasticism seems to have weakened the evangelical spirit. The church was busy trying to heal her own wounds. There was, however, some work among the Muslim by St. Francis and his disciples, and extension of the effort among the Mongols of Persia, China, and part of Russia. These missions were only passively supported by the church, and were opposed from without, so the work was not lasting, and some opportunities offered the church were never accepted.

There were some strong Nestorian churches in China under the Khans, with headquarters in the capital, Cambaluc (Peking). In 1274 there was a special ministry under Kublai Khan to supervise the Christians, and in 1330 there were reported to be 30,000 Christians in China, with scattered outposts in Tibet and other surrounding areas. Meanwhile the Catholic Church was roused to interest in the East through some of its crusades. Some early attempts to enter China ended in failure. The first to arrive were the merchants Nicolo and Mathaei Polo. They returned as an embassy from Kublai Khan to the Pope requesting missionaries. When they arrived in Syria there was a papal interregnum. The request was placed before Pope Gregory X in 1271, immediately after he had ascended the throne. The charge given the ambassadors by the Khan was:

> You shall go to your High Priest and shall pray him on our behalf to send me a hundred men skilled in your religion . . . and so I shall be baptized, and when I shall be baptized all my barons and great men will be baptized, and then their subjects will receive baptism, and so there will be more Christians here than there in your parts.[5]

A few missionaries were sent, among them a Franciscan, John of Montecorvino, who went by way of India, spending some time preaching the Gospel in that country. He arrived in Cambaluc in 1294.

> Although vigorously opposed by the Nestorians he remained in the capital and won the favor of the court. By 1300 he had completed, so he says, a church with a bell tower and three bells. He had, by 1305, baptized about six thousand converts; he had bought a hundred and fifty young boys of pagan parents, had baptized them, had taught them Greek and Latin, and had written out for them the psalter, thirty hymnaries, and two breviaries. Eleven of the boys had learned the service and took turns in helping in it.[6]

John was appointed archbishop of Cambaluc, and other missionaries were sent out as bishops of other areas of China. Reports from 1318 indicate that 20,000 foreigners in Cambaluc had been won for the faith and that there were other cities also where the church was flourishing.

After the death of John in 1330, a few other missionaries were sent to China, but some never reached their destination. Europe was impoverished by the Black Death. Wars made travel to China hazardous. The Mongol empire was broken up. Under the Ming dynasty there was suppression of Christianity and China was closed to missionaries.

There was new interest in China in the sixteenth century, under the inspiration of the great missionary Xavier. He was a student in Paris in 1528 when Loyola, then 37, limped into the city. Xavier and Loyola met and became fast friends; Loyola had a great deal of influence on Xavier.

> Years afterwards, when Benedict Palmio set down his memories of his talks with Ignatius, he recorded that the great sculptor of men had said that the hardest block he ever encountered was, at least in the beginning, young Francis Xavier.[7]

When Loyola established the Jesuit order, Xavier was one of the original members. They intended to go to the Holy Land, but in 1540 Xavier and a companion went to India with papal authorization and the admonition, "Go and set all on fire." While in India he met Angero, a refugee from Japan who interested him in that country. He worked in Japan for a while with some success, but recognizing that the culture of Japan and much of the religious influence there had come from China, he determined to go there. He came to the island of Sancian off the coast of China, and found that the mainland was closed. He prayed and planned for work in that country, but died on the island December 3, 1552.

The church continued to have interest in China and other Jesuits were sent there. In 1578 Ruggieri was sent. He prepared himself for the work on the island of Macao, and he was finally able to establish himself on the mainland with Matteo Ricci who became the outstanding early Jesuit missionary in China.

After several attempts, Ricci was able to start work in the capital, mostly among the officials and literati. He won the favor of the emperor with gifts of clocks and musical instruments, with his mathematical and astronomical knowledge, by providing maps, charts, and correct calendars for the court, by assuming the Chinese dress of a scholar and becoming versed in Chinese literature and philosophy. His companion, Adam Schoal, worked with him in these ventures and they were able to make some corrections in the Chinese record of time. Schoal also built a foundry and provided cannon for the Chinese army, each one marked with a cross! In a short time there were 120,000 converts. By 1700 there were said to have been 300,000 Christians in nine different provinces and the Jesuits were influential in court enjoying support of the emperor. Times changed, however, and the edict of 1724 proscribed Christianity in the empire. There were several reasons for the failure of the mission.

1. The Chinese leaders were afraid of political interference from foreign courts through the Jesuits. This fear was possibly aroused by the prestige won by the missionaries through their activities, and because of their tendency to use external influence in their work. The Chinese were also fearful lest affiliation with the church might place them under the law of the pope instead of under the law of the emperor.

2. The Jesuits did everything they could to accommodate their religion to the people among whom they worked.

> Thus, the Christians were allowed to expose their ancestor tablets, to burn candles and incense before them, to make the usual prostrations, and to invoke the intercession of the dead: they might also continue to venerate Confucius, provided they refrained from worship and sacrifices.[8]

There was rapid growth of the church, and in 1651 the missionaries planned to erect a patriarchate in China with three archdioceses and twelve dioceses. By this time the Franciscans and Dominicans who had been conducting a flourishing mission work in the Philippines came to China. They challenged the accommodating policies of the Jesuits. The "rites controversy" broke out, split the church, and was brought before Chinese officials. Accused before Rome of practicing idolatry, the Jesuits were condemned in 1632 for their policy. These proceedings naturally weakened the prestige of the Church.

3. Another controversy was that pertaining to the correct name to use for God. The Dominicans chose the term *T'ien Chu* (Lord of Heaven). The Jesuits had used the terms *T'ien* (God, or Heaven) and *Shang ti* (Ruler over All). The Jesuits went to the government in Peking, and the Dominicans went to Rome, for authority in reaching a settlement. The Chinese were disturbed by the ferocity of this discussion. The pope ruled in favor of the Dominicans and stated that no one could go to China who did not abide by this de-

cision. The emperor took the other view and ruled that no one could come who did not use *his* choice of terms.

4. There was, of course, constant opposition from leaders of the Chinese religions who also had friends among the emperor's followers and officials. The opposition had broken out openly on several occasions. Their hands were now strengthened and the result was the proscription of Christianity.

Catholic mission work in India actually began with the exploitation by Vasco da Gama when he sailed from Portugal with a fleet of ships in 1497. Settling at Goa and founding a colony along the coast, he was under commission to Christianize the people as he conquered the new territory for Portugal. Every ship that came out carried monks and lay missionaries. Goa was made an archbishropic in 1557. The method of "Christianizing" was almost equivalent to announcing allegiance to Portugal and the result was a group of nominal Christians changed in few ways, if any, from their heathen past. In 1538 the low-caste Paravas living south of Goa promised to become Christian if the Portuguese army would protect them from the ravages of the Moslems who periodically raided the coast. Eighty-five deputies were baptized in Goa at the time of the negotiations, and made the promise for all their people. A fleet was sent to assist them and in a few weeks there were 20,000 who had been baptized. No previous instruction had been given them and no teachers were left to train them in the Faith.

When Xavier came in 1542 he remained a while in Goa and began negotiations to have a training school (started by the monks there) transferred to the Jesuit order—negotiations which later were successful. Finding it difficult to reach the pagan groups, he started his work among the Christians—presumably the Thomas Christians. He then went south, and worked among the Paravas.

> In his shabby loba, and barefoot (for his shoes had worn out), he went from village to village over the burning plains. At each place he stood under his umbrella baptizing all day long until his arms ached, while one of his Tamil assistants made out with a stylus upon a strip of almyra-palm the certificate of baptism. In one month he baptized ten thousand people, and in all during his mission in southern India he must have baptized thirty thousand. His conversion of the Paravas, it is pointed out by Pere Lhande, is the only instance of an entire caste being brought into the Church.[9]

Xavier did not learn the language of the people, but relied on interpreters. He sought the help of Indians who knew some Portuguese, prepared a summary of the Christian faith (which was poorly translated), and left a copy in the places he visited. He would preach a time or two and then baptize the people.

> Whether any real understanding of fundamental truths was thereby attained, or whether Xavier could make what he said sufficiently comprehensible even to the Christians, owing to his incompetent interpreters, cannot now be determined. It sometimes happened that a whole village would be baptized in a single day, and thirty villages were soon reckoned as belonging to the Christian community.[10]

Xavier was not averse to using political and military means to advance his mission. At one time he plotted with the opponents of the king on the island of Manar to have their ruler dethroned by Portuguese forces and have his challenger on the mainland enthroned in his place on condition that the inhabitants would all consent to be baptized. For some reason this plot was never carried out. Xavier was in India not longer than two and a half years. After his departure for Japan, other missionaries continued to work in India.

Xavier had been very successful among the low caste people, but felt frustrated before the educated Brahmins. Robert Nobili, who arrived in 1605, a brilliant man who could preach in the language of the people after six months' stay in the country, wished to reach the Brahmins. Paul had said that a man should be a Jew to the Jews and a Greek to the Greeks. Nobili decided to be a Brahmin to the Brahmins. He appeared in Madura as a Brahmin ascetic. He studied Telegu, could preach in Tamil, and also studied Sanskrit and the sacred books written in that language. He proclaimed himself to be a sadhu and a Roman rajah. He lived like a guru (Hindu teacher) and adopted a vegetarian diet. He went further and produced an "ancient" discolored parchment to prove that he was a Roman Brahmin of the highest caste, and wrote books in which he grafted and modified Christian doctrines on a Hindu foundation. The most notable of such efforts was the forging of a "Fifth Veda," which he claimed came truly from heaven. This forgery was accepted as a true veda for 150 years. He permitted the converts to retain their old customs and practices and admitted only Brahmins to his meals. He had quite a following, but then difficulties arose from several quarters.

His very success caused opposition as the old Brahmins under their leaders resented this new thrust into the old ways. His converts were puzzled when they met Christians from other areas of the realm who followed an entirely different life, admitting that they had given up caste when they became Christian. His own ecclesiastical authorities noted the discrepancies between his method and the normal Christian approach and condemned them. His archbishop defended him, however, so he was permitted to continue his work, with some modification of methods, till he retired. The number of his converts has been listed by some as one thousand, and by others in the general term "thousands."

A somewhat similar method was employed by Joseph Beschi who reached India in 1710. His main goal was to reach the literati.

> If Hinduism has its ascetics, it has also its high priests who live in luxurious comfort, and whose outward surroundings are marked by pomp and circumstance. This was the line chosen by Beschi: by magnificence he would dazzle the people. When he traveled it was in a costly palanquin. In advance went an attendant bearing an umbrella of purple silk, at each side ran servants with gorgeous fans of peacock feathers, and in the palanquin, upon a splendid tiger-skin and clad in rich and picturesque robes, reclined the mighty Guru.[11]

No doubt these men were zealous for their cause, but the Jesuits were suppressed in Portugal in 1759 and were deported from India. Some converts retained their faith. About 60,000 apostatized to Islam. Others returned to the Hindu religion.

Xavier's work in Japan was also of rather brief duration. In 1549 he arrived there with two other missionaries and the Japanese whom he had baptized in India and given the name Christian Paul. Xavier landed with lofty motives of Christianizing the people by preaching, but at the same time he tried to make arrangements to serve as the agent of a Portuguese merchant so that he might proceed with the prestige of a business man. They began preaching in front of a Buddhist monastery, teaching the people from a book he had prepared. They also tried street preaching.

The next day, without waiting for any order or permission of the king, Father Francis decided that we should preach in the streets of Aamaguchi. This we did in the following manner. We stood at the crossings where the people were abundant. I first read from the book an account of the creation of the world. Then in a loud voice I spoke of the great sins committed by the Japanese, dwelling principally on three things: First they forgot God, the Creator and the all-powerful one, who made and preserves them. Instead of Him they adored wood, stone and the inanimate things, through them worshipping the devil, who is the enemy of God and men. In the second place, they give themselves up to the abominations of Sodom; and at this point I exposed the shame and baseness of sin, speaking of the chastisements with which the world has been afflicted because of it. The third sin was that of the women, who, to spare themselves the trouble of bringing up children, slay their offspring at birth or even before, an act that proves them guilty of horrible cruelty and inhumanity. While I was thus preaching, Father Francis at my side engaged in prayer, asking God to bless my words to those that listened.[12]

Seeking to get to the emperor, Xavier proceeded to Kyoto. Fernandez describes his entrance into the city.

Wearing a Siamese hat, Francis almost danced into Kyoto, in the wildest high spirits. The Japanese, Bernard, adds that he kept throwing an apple high into the air and running forward to catch it. Those in the Daimyo's entourage must have thought him mad—this lanky scarecrow with bleeding feet, laughing and shouting as though he were a boy. Never before or since has a Papal Nuncio entered the capital of a great nation this way.[13]

Not gaining entrance because he failed to take gifts along to give to the underlings through whom he had to work to see the emperor, he learned that he must change his approach. He gave presents, dressed as one of the scholarly Japanese, and, to gain prestige, used an escort of Portuguese naval officers when entering a city.

When he left Japan after two and a half years, there were possibly a few thousand converts. Other Jesuits continued the work with some success and some setbacks. The succeeding history of this early venture became complicated with political involvements and international relations. The result was that Christianity was proscribed by successive decrees in 1612 and 1614. Christians were massacred and churches destroyed. For two hundred and fifty years Japan was hermetically sealed against all foreign contact. When Perry reopened Japan to the West it was marvelous to find that some thousand Christians had persisted in the faith and had handed it down in secret to their children.

Not all the missions begun during this period were ill-fated. Some of them were successful and were continued into modern times. The examples given, however, dramatically illustrate some of the methods used in an earlier period.

1. There was dependence upon explorers to missionize various countries they entered. Henry the Navigator was commissioned to take the lands he discovered in the name of the church as well as in the name of his emperor. The same was true of Columbus and succeeding explorers in the Americas. In Goa there was an effort to bring the people not only under the power of Portugal, but under the Pope as well. This formal accession to the church did not mean the conversion of the people to the faith, except where spiritual work was done among them later.

2. There was direct preaching of the Word of God. There was much use of the Old Testament in an attempt to awaken recognition of God as the Creator of the world and all men, and to give awareness of the Law of God. This was followed by the Gospel. In the mass conversions, it was impossible to make any careful presentation of either the Law or the Gospel.

3. The Sacrament of Baptism was often administered without adequate instruction.

4. There was a very definite plan to work from the top down. Kings, emperors, official classes, and educated people were sought first, wherever this was possible, to give prestige to the message. It was felt that the influence from these people would be useful in reaching the lower classes.

5. Free use of artifice, the attractiveness of Western culture and the marvels of Western inventions were used as tools to gain entry to a country.

6. At times the church was presented as a powerful organization with all possible pomp in order to make it appealing to the people.

7. Accommodation to the customs and the faith of the people among whom they worked was common practice. This was frowned on by some members of the church but was found useful in avoiding offense usually caused by the proclamation to people who are polytheistic.

8. The tendency to put reliance on temporal support was carried over into this period, with varied results.

The key to understanding the general approach of this period is given by Muelder in speaking of the Indian missions. There was an attempt to make Christ indigenous to the history, background, and culture of the people. Christ was not presented as one coming with a different religion, but as one who fulfilled their own religions. With this attempt, pagan religion was not discarded. The "natural religion" was considered to be of God, with no basic opposition to Christianity in it. It needed only purification and completion which could be found in the church. Those who had been faithful in their past pagan religion, according to some missionary interpretation, might, through their sincerity, have seen Christ.

> The ancient "holy men" of India were considered to be "saved." This "salvation" was acknowledged to be theirs by dint of their zealous practice of the religion they knew, even though they had no relationship with Christ. Based on the desire of God to save all men, it was declared that their sincerity implied a desire to use the Christian means of grace if they had been available, and this desire was taken in lieu of the deed. They were, therefore, considered to be members of God's Kingdom by adoption.

Following this policy resulted in the wide assimilation of past pagan teachings, methods, and practices into the missionary churches of the time. The main doctrines of the church were firmly held; but other doctrines that were truly not compatible were permitted to exist side by side with them. The insistence that salvation was not complete without the church was never relinquished. The church was, however, willing to absorb individuals, groups, or classes of people on the basis of mental assent, without much change from the past, in the tacit understanding that their acceptance of the church was an admission that they needed it to fulfill their faith. There were even instances when the church accepted personages of pagan religions as saints—on the supposition that they now knew that their incomplete faith of the past was complete only in the Christ of the church.

In the fifteenth and sixteenth centuries a new era of missions began with the discovery of America. The sword of the conquistador and the cross of the missionary were introduced simultaneously into the new soil which was claimed for the pontiff of Rome and the kings of Portugal and Spain. By public decree, every ship bearing explorers to the new land had to bear at least one priest. The Pope also sent groups of missionaries, at the request of Charles, to evangelize the newly won territory.

Some missionaries willingly used the prestige and power that this close connection with the conquistador provided. Others found that the treatment meted out to the natives by the explorers proved a handicap to them in their missionary work, and sought to withdraw from military force and gold hunters. The conquest for Latin America was ruthless and bloody and, as the priests accompanied the men who dealt in cruelty, it was difficult to disassociate themselves from them. To the soldiers the objective was gold, and methods used in securing it were not governed by a spirit of humanitarianism. One of the more dramatic instances of ruthlessness was the incident between Pizarro, conqueror of Peru, and the Inca ruler Atahaulpa. When the Spaniards entered Peru they were met with friendliness, but the action of the conquerors aroused opposition. The Spaniards retaliated by killing all who opposed them and taking what they wanted for themselves. On meeting Atahaulpa, they gave him a Bible. He threw this on the ground and demanded that they replace the property they had taken from the storehouses en route. The king was taken captive, and several thousand of his subjects were slain. He began negotiating for his release and the Spaniards demanded a roomful of gold as ransom. This was provided. Instead of releasing him, they tried him on several charges ranging from adultery and murder to idolatry and rebellion. He was condemned to die. The only freedom he received was a choice between being beheaded or dying by strangulation. He was baptized and publicly executed on August 29, 1533.

This was not the only method of approach used in "Christianizing" the people. Some priests objected strenuously to the use of government force.

What little was done toward education and improving the lot of the Indians was the work, not of the colonial governments, but of the Jesuits and other religious orders, whose efforts were far greater and far more humanitarian than those of the Church as a whole.[14]

Several of them took up the cudgel on behalf of the Indian. In 1542 Emperor Charles abolished the "encomienda system" whereby a colonist was given a certain number of Indians as virtual slaves on the condition that he would train them for work and teach them the Christian faith. This practice had too often been abused. The priests were to learn the native language of the people, train them, and provide them with Christian literature. In some areas, especially in the Parana area of Venezuela reaching in toward Colombia, the priests started special settlements for the natives where they could organize and supervise villages of Christians. The salary of the priests and special grants were given by the government, but a tax was paid by each individual. This method was not ideal. It separated the Christians from the rest of the people and made them dependent on a patriarchal system under control of a priest. On the other hand, it protected them from the depredations of the colonists.

For a while the natives were under the dual control of Spain (or Portugal) and the government organized by the conquistadores and the colonists. When republics were established, the nature of the churches remained unchanged. Spiritual colonialism continued, and for a long time very little was done to train native leadership. As late as 1576 official orders were in effect, prohibiting ordination of Mestizos and Indians. The first Indian priests were ordained in 1794. The council in Lima in 1552 decided to administer only three sacraments to the Indians, namely baptism, matrimony, and penance. It was a long time before they were admitted to communion, and then only once a year at Easter.

In many areas the church in Latin America is still primitive. It has on several occasions been severely criticized by Catholics from the United States. A report from Catholic sources in Brazil states that only six per cent of the women and four per cent of the men are active members of the church. In Bolivia some religious processions of the Catholics have figures of the Virgin Mary and large emblems of the old Inca Sun God carried side by side. Uruguay has been called an agnostic country where the church provides services for the minority of the people though it lays claim to all.

The influence of church and state are intertwined in many, if not all, countries of Latin America. The prime example is Colombia where, as a rule, through a long history, the church has been able to dictate to the state. Persecution of Protestants has been a joint venture of church and state. Priests have immunity before the law and are given special favors. Areas in the lowlands toward the north and in Parana are called "mission areas" where only Catholics have a right to do mission work, and this work is supported by the state. In many areas the church does not reach the people regularly. In some urban areas there is a high degree of ecclesiastical development with cathedrals, monasteries, and seminaries.[15]

The church was dominant in the economic and political affairs of Mexico until the revolution. All church properties were nationalized as a protest, but indirectly, through high government officials, the church has gradually reestablished a rather dominant control.

Educational standards are generally low. Some fine universities have been erected, but they are few. In many countries, literacy falls below the fifty per cent mark. In Colombia the national university is controlled by the church. Up to recent years Protestants have been excluded from its classes. Catholic services are compulsory in the elementary schools even where there may be Protestant pupils.

South America is an important study in the field of missions. Remnants of methods from the Early Catholic Mission Period still exist. Bridging the gap from the more primitive to the more modern mission methods is taking a long time, and the changes can be noted and studied as they take place.

CHAPTER TEN

MISSION AND THE REFORMATION

One would expect that the Reformers and their followers, with their emphasis on the Word of God, would also have seen the necessity of supplying this Word to people of lands other than those immediately affected by the Reformation. This, however, was not true. Critics have often asked why Luther and his associates did not begin mission work. There were possibly several reasons.

1. For a period of 500 years (roughly 1000-1500), missionary efforts had been weak and sporadic, and finally abandoned altogether as an activity of the Roman Church. The Reformation church had no strong example of mission responsibility to follow. It was not until 1541, twenty-four years after the beginning of the Reformation, that the first serious Catholic missionary program was begun by the Jesuit order. In 1622 when Gregory, the first Jesuit Pope, was elected, the Catholic Church officially took up active mission work by forming the Society for the Propagation of the Faith.

2. The Reformation came at approximately the same time that the period of great exploration began. The newly discovered lands belonged to Catholic nations. The Church of the Reformation had no access to them. Germany was a rather self-enclosed nation, and England was not yet a maritime power. The early missionary efforts were stimulated first by a sense of Christian responsibility for colonists and only for the colonies.

3. The young churches of the Reformation were busy establishing their own organizations and had neither ecclesiastical orders nor

training centers for producing missionaries. The German *Landes-kirche*, the establishment of the church in smaller geographical areas under the protection of a prince or ruler, became a block to the outward expansion of the church.

4. The Protestant churches were fighting for their rights until 1648 when the Peace of Westphalia provided assurance of their survival.

In spite of these difficulties and hindrances, Luther did have a concept of the need for missions in his day. In stating his convictions he went counter to the current thoughts of his day. The "Great Commission" was thought to have been fulfilled in the Apostolic era so that it no longer applied to the Church. Luther made reply to this interpretation in an Ascension Day sermon based on Mark 16:14-20.

> A question arises about this passage, "go ye into all the world," as to how it is to be understood, since the apostles certainly did not visit all the world. No apostle came hither to us; and many a heathen island has since been discovered, where the Gospel has never been preached. Yet the Scriptures say: "Their sound went out into all the earth." Rom. 10, 18. Answer: Their preaching went out into all the world, although it has not yet come into all the world. This going out has been begun and continues, although it is not yet completed; the Gospel, however, will be preached even farther and wider, until the judgment day. When this preaching shall have reached all parts of the world, and shall have been everywhere heard, then will the message be complete and its mission accomplished; then will the last day also be at hand.
>
> The preaching of this message may be likened to a stone thrown into the water, producing ripples which circle outward from it, the waves rolling always on and on, one driving the other, till they come to the shore. Although the center becomes quiet, the waves do not rest, but move forward. So it is with the preaching of the Word. It was begun by the apostles, and it constantly goes forward, is pushed on farther and farther by the preachers, driven hither and thither into the world, yet always being made known to those who never heard it before. . . .[1]

Besides the implication that the Gospel will naturally spread from one age to the other and from one area to the other, he is clear in his teaching that messengers must be sent with the Gospel if the desired result is to be actualized. In his meditation on Psalm 117 Luther writes:

> Now if all heathen are to praise God, this assumes that He has become their God. If He is to be their God, then they must know Him, believe in Him, and give up all idolatry. One cannot praise God with an idolatrous mouth or an unbelieving heart. And if they are to believe, they must first hear His word and thereby receive the Holy Spirit, who through faith purifies and enlightens their hearts. One cannot come to faith or lay hold on the Holy Spirit without hearing the Word first, as St. Paul has said (Rom. 10:14): "How are they to believe in Him of whom they have never heard?" and (Gal. 3:2): "You have received the Spirit through the proclamation of faith." If they are to hear His word, then preachers must be sent to proclaim God's Word to them; for not all the heathen can come to Jerusalem . . . "[2]

The Turks were, at this time, the closest non-Christian people to the Germans, and Luther urged that the Christians seek to bring them to the faith of Jesus Christ, specially mentioning the opportunity of those serving as slaves of the Turks to so serve that they might, in their capacity as slaves, become preachers of the Gospel. He reached beyond the Turks in his specific admonition that the people should use the languages of the people with whom they have contact in the proclamation of the Gospel.

> I am not at all in sympathy with those who cling to one language and despise all others. I would rather train the youth and folks who could also be of service to Christ in foreign lands and able to converse with the natives there, in order to avoid the experience of the Waldensians in Bohemia, who confined their faith to one language so completely, that they cannot speak correctly and intelligently with anyone, unless he first speaks their language. This was not the method of the Holy Spirit at the beginning. He did not tarry until all the world came to Jerusalem and studied Hebrew, but gave manifold tongues for the office of the ministry, so that the apostles could preach wherever they went. I would rather follow this example. It is proper that the youth should be trained in many languages, for who knows how God may use them in time to come.[3]

The fact that mission work was not begun by Luther and his contemporaries was not primarily because of policy or doctrine, but because of other circumstances that governed the nations in which

Reformation churches developed. It is significant that Luther's Catechism, the Augsburg Confession, and other Luther writings were translated into the language of the Crots and Wends eleven years after Luther's death in an effort to reach the Turks with the Gospel. Four years later Gustav Vasa of Sweden appointed a missionary to work among the Lapps. Sweden was at that time the only Lutheran country with a "heathen possession," and the extensive work carried out there was the first real missionary effort by Lutherans.

The period immediately following the Reformation also had its challenge. At the end of the sixteenth century the Reformers were attacked by the Catholic Church for not having done anything to convert the Jews or the Turks. R. Vellarminus wrote a scathing attack stating that the Lutherans compared themselves to the apostles and evangelists, while they had won less than a handful of Jews from among their own midst or Turks in Poland and Hungary.

The leaders of the Reformation found it difficult to answer this attack. Some reasoned that they should have missions, and would when the way was open for them. Others maintained that the Great Commission was given to the Apostles and no longer applied to the church. Those who did see the need of missions and were ready to act upon their convictions had to face the opposition of the majority.

It was only after the Dutch and English had begun to establish colonial empires that there were openings for a strong mission program. The Dutch had possessions in Indonesia and Ceylon, and a short outline of the Christian faith was prepared for sailors traveling to the Far East to use in missionary work. The Dutch East Indies Company, under pressure of the churches, established a seminary in Leyden and, between 1622 and 1633, trained twelve pastors who were to serve the Dutch colonists and evangelize the natives in Dutch territories. By the end of the seventeenth century there were 10,000 Christians in Java and 40,000 in Ambon. Much of this work was superficial because, at the beginning, a minister received a cash bonus for each person baptized. There were, however, some lasting results. The entire New Testament was translated into Malay in 1688. The Dutch also had very effective work in Taiwan until they were driven out by Chinese pirates in 1661.

One of the first men to arouse missionary interest among the churches of the Reformation was an Austrian, Baron von Welz. He is spoken of as one who "formed the mold in which modern missions took shape." In a series of pamphlets he set forth the missionary duties of the church and requested that a society be organized for the extension of the Gospel among the heathen and for founding a college to train missionaries. He used the classic approach to arouse the conscience of the Christians by asking if it were right for them to hold the Gospel for themselves, to have so many pastors for their own churches, and to spend so much money on themselves when others were lacking the message of God's saving grace. Meeting reproaches and ridicule, he decided to act on his own. He proceeded to Holland, was ordained as an apostle to the Gentiles, and set sail for Dutch Guinea at his own expense. He died as a martyr to the inhospitable climate of the area and the apparent failure of the mission. But his writings and his courageous action took on new importance. His death spoke clearly and loudly to the church to assume its missionary obligation.

One missionary of this period became a true forerunner of the Protestant mission era. Mission zeal was stimulated as the story of his sacrificial work became known in Europe and as the final results of his efforts were published.

Hans Egede, a pastor in Norway, had heard of the colonizing and evangelizing work of Leif the Lucky in Greenland, and the subsequent neglect of this area by the church. Against much opposition he sailed from Bergen with forty-six colonists in 1721. He expected to find remnants of the early Norwegian colonists there, but found only unlettered Eskimos. He and the colonists with him suffered great difficulty and privation, and the Eskimos were not receptive to the Gospel. Undaunted, Egede and his wife learned the Eskimo language and began a program of evangelization. The colonists were called back to Norway, but with a few who remained with him, the work continued on a reduced scale, and they founded the model colony of *Godthaab* (Good Hope).

August 21, 1732, the first Moravian missionaries left for the island of St. Thomas in the West Indies. Six months later three Moravian missionaries were sent to Greenland. There was little contact between the missions there because the Moravians had little confidence in Egede and did not consider him a converted Christian. This saddened Egede for he had hoped these brethren would provide help in the mission work. Each group worked separately, struggling to win people to the Gospel, in neighboring areas.

A Christian family from Greenland had been sent to Norway and Denmark for a brief stay. On their way back it proved that they had contracted smallpox. Only one child survived and he seemed healthy on arrival in Greenland, but he soon took sick and died. A smallpox plague swept through the settlements, and between two and three thousand died. Hans Egede and his wife Gertrud labored incessantly among the sick and dying, visiting all they could reach and making their home a hospital for all who could be crowded in. The people's attitude toward the Gospel thawed as they saw this service of Christian love.[4]

> A Greenlander who, while strong and healthy, had not cared about the instruction of the minister, nay, had even met it with derision, when dying bore witness to his goodness in the following pathetic words: "You have been more kind to us than we have been to one another; you have fed us, when we famished; you have buried our dead, who would else have been a prey to dogs, foxes and ravens, and in particular you have told us of God and how to become blessed, so that we may now die gladly, in expectation of a better life hereafter."[5]

This was the beginning of the Christianization of Greenland. Hans Egede, his two sons, and other successors continued the work until the entire island was considered a Christian country.

CHAPTER ELEVEN

THE DANISH-HALLE MISSION

The arrival of William Carey in India in 1793 is usually considered the beginning of the modern Protestant mission era. In setting this date, all earlier efforts of the Dutch and other colonial powers and mission societies have been ignored. This is partly justifiable, since most earlier efforts of bringing Christ to other nations were either short-lived or restricted to colonies of the countries from which the missionaries came. Some of the workers were chaplains to a colony rather than missionaries.

One early Protestant mission that should not be ignored, however, was the Danish-Halle Mission. Its methods, results, and influence upon the Protestant Christian world set the pattern that has been followed by missionaries and missions of the modern era. When the Danish-Halle Mission movement began, the church had developed a cold, rationalistic spirit that had weakened its message to the people and quenched mission interest. The emphasis was on "orthodoxy."

> Aberrations from the norm of orthodoxy were to be answered by instruments of logic alone. Stiff formalism carried into the pulpit learned disputes far above the understanding of ordinary men. The religious experts forgot a deep, wise saying of Luther: "The heart of religion lies in its personal pronouns." No attempt was made to meet the real needs of the layman or to supply an outlet for his emotions. He existed just to be indoctrinated![1]

There were several attempts to correct this situation in the church, but it was not until Philip Jakob Spener (1635-1705) began the pietist movement in Germany with the publishing of his *Pia Desideria* (1675) that the church was brought back to a vital life of Gospel witness. His movement was thoroughly biblical and faithful to the confessions of the church. There was stress on a living manifestation of the faith that differed from the worldly life, an emphasis on Bible study, and an effort to bridge the gap between clergy and laity by stressing the priesthood of all believers. One of the books that had greatly influenced him in forming his theology was Johann Arndt's *True Christianity*. This book had been a wholesome leaven during the time of extreme orthodoxy and had survived that period. His good friend August Hermann Francke (1663-1727), a scholar and professor at Halle, backed the pietist movement and aided its progress.

> Francke's work at Halle was a conspicuous success. There he preached and lectured from 1694 to 1727. Between 800 and 1200 divinity students passed through his hands annually— the record for the universities of Germany. The clergy of Prussia, compelled to study at royal Halle, were steadily leavened with a spirit that was Biblical rather than Confessional. Francke valued "a drop of true love more than a sea of knowledge. . . . Our aim must be not to build up *scientia*, but rather *conscientia*." He believed that if the Bible was widely read by the laity, Luther's dream would come true.[2]

It was through the direct work of Francke that many of the welfare institutions were established in Germany. He encouraged the founding of a school for training missionaries to the Jews. It was he who sent H. M. Muhlenberg to organize the Lutheran Church in North America.

Under the leadership of Spener and Francke the pietist movement awakened in people a missionary zeal which, at the time, was scorned by the clergy. The key results of their influence were the Danish-Halle Mission and the work of Count von Zinzendorf, who later became the leader of Moravian missions. From these beginnings the Protestants of Germany, Scandinavia, and England were stimulated to begin their great missionary enterprises.

King Frederick IV of Denmark, who had been concerned about bringing the Gospel to non-Christian lands, decided to begin his work in the Danish colonies at Tranquebar, India. He commanded his church officials to find men for this purpose, but received no favorable response either from them or from the Danish clergy. No men were found who were willing to go as missionaries. Dr. Luetkens, German chaplain to the Danish court, was then given the task of finding missionaries, and he received the assignment with enthusiasm. He turned to his friends in Berlin who stated that there were men there ready to be sent. Calls were sent to two men, Heinrich Pluetschau and Bartholomaeus Ziegenbalg. Before they could be ordained in Denmark, they had to pass a theological examination given by the church officials. Both of them failed (possibly by predetermination of the examiners), but by court orders were given a new examination which they both passed (possibly by predetermination of the court). They were ordained by the bishop of the Danish Church. They arrived in Tranquebar on July 9, 1706, and immediately began work among the Tamil-speaking people. They learned the language, conducted schools, preached, and produced Christian literature and literature concerning India that would help future missionaries coming to work in the country. The New Testament was translated by 1715. A hymnbook for use in schools and church services was published the same year. Ziegenbalg began translating the Old Testament and had gone as far as the Book of Ruth when others took over and completed the work. Congregations were organized, and a seminary was founded for training Indian pastors and church leaders.

Ziegenbalg's work drew a great deal of attention in Germany, Scandinavia, England, and the young churches in America. Mission zeal was being awakened. The Anglican Society for the Propagation of the Gospel in Foreign Parts, founded in 1701, sent funds in 1712 for the purchase of a printing press. The Germans later sent a second press, a font of Tamil type, and two men to run the press. Ziegenbalg returned to Denmark in 1714 and traveled extensively in Denmark and Germany stimulating mission interest within the churches. He was received with enthusiasm wherever he went.

The king of Denmark gave continued support to the work, and later organized a mission board to be in contact with the missionaries. But the policies of the board were not always wise. Their demands for extreme privation on the part of the missionaries, and failure to supply sufficient funds for the necessary expansion of the work may have hastened the death of Ziegenbalg. He died in 1719. Other missionaries from Germany came to fill vacancies and increase the staff. The most famous of these was Christian Frederick Schwartz. He too had been trained by Francke, and was stirred to deeper mission interest by a missionary named Schultze, who had been invalided during service and was forced to return to Germany. Schwartz was ordained with two others in Copenhagen in 1749 and arrived in India July 13, 1750.

Modern mission methods, begun under Pluetschau and Ziegenbalg, were more fully developed under Schwartz. He was a brilliant man. He was able to preach in the Tamil language after only four months on the field. He studied the sacred books of India in order to better understand and reach the people with the Gospel. In 1760 he worked for five months in Ceylon. In 1762 he preached in Tanjore and Trichinopoly and was heard by the rajah of Tanjore. The rajah became a trusted friend and was helped in many ways by Schwartz.

Conscious of the financial stringency of the mission, and feeling its restrictions, Schwartz accepted a leave of absence to work under the British mission, the Society for the Propagation of Christian Knowledge, which received financial support from the Madras government. There he served as chaplain to the English garrison, where his services became so popular that larger quarters had to be provided. A building seating 1,500 people was erected, and was paid for by popular subscription. He also worked among the Indians, organizing a congregation in Trichinopoly. He was comparatively well paid, but lived frugally and gave a large portion of his salary to his fellow missionaries in the Danish mission.

His extensive efforts in the area of relief and his interested concern for the welfare of the people won him the confidence of government and people alike. During a period of political trouble he gathered supplies to insure sufficient food for the people who had lost confidence in the rajah. Many had moved out of the realm. Schwartz persuaded traders to bring in a thousand bullocks to provide food for those near starvation. At his request, over a thousand people returned in a day. When the rajah died, Schwartz was made guardian for his son, the heir apparent to the throne. He reorganized the government, restored the son to office when it had been usurped by a pretender, and won the gratitude of the people of the realm.

Schwartz's literary work was extensive. He developed self-supporting congregations, unified the church, and practiced the best type of economic relief by teaching the people to aid themselves. He was firmly enthroned in the hearts of both English and Indians.

When Schwartz died in 1794 the pioneer period of the mission was over. In 1740 there were 5,600 Christians. By the beginning of the nineteenth century there were 15,000 Christians. After his death, there was a decline in support from Denmark. Rationalism spread over Europe. G. C. Knapp, editing the mission periodical, wrote:

> The future of the mission depends on the sending of more workers . . . but we can no longer find qualified men to serve as missionaries who love their God and love their brethren. Let us, therefore, rather die than send out wolves who destroy the flock much more quickly.[3]

Denmark's alliance with Napoleon caused England to take Tranquebar in 1808. The Society for the Propagation of Christian Knowledge transferred all its work in India to the Society for the Propagation of the Gospel. In 1824 the Danish colonial officers decided to discontinue the mission and retain only the schools. The last Danish pastor left Tranquebar in 1847. During the history of this early mission 36,970 souls had been won to the Christian faith.

> At the plenary session of the Lutheran Federation in Hannover in 1952 the Rev. Joel Lakra in the official report gave the following opinion about the result of the Tranquebar Mission: "The only mistake which was made at this time . . . was to miss the opportunity to establish an indigenous Church, which could thrust firm roots into the soil of India. The result of this was that when the number of Lutheran missionaries gradually decreased, the majority of the newly converted Lutherans joined other missions such as the Church Missionary Society of England."

> One can look at it in this way. Perhaps the decline would not have taken place if, in spite of the prevailing conditions and great difficulties, an independent and self-supporting Church had been built up. The very virtues of the Tranquebar missionaries became a cause for many mistakes. Fully appreciating the problems of the pioneers and without doing the missionaries an injustice, one can say that the mission was too much like an anxious mother keeping her grown-up daughter under her supervision as long as possible without training her to stand on her

own feet. The times and the circumstances make it clear to us why they did not go far enough, according to our modern ideas, in the direction of spontaneous expansion, self-government, and self-support. If the tie to a mission with its roots in Europe had not been so strong among the workers, in the management, and in finances, an autonomous Church would have come about and the disintegration of the substantial results of the Tranquebar mission might perhaps have been avoided. Finally, the causes lay outside of India.[4]

During the decline of the official Danish mission, a Lutheran mission society had been formed in the Dresden area, in 1836, which continued as the Leipzig mission. What was left of the work at Tranquebar was turned over to the Evangelical Lutheran Mission in Dresden in April 1846. The Tamil Christians concurred in this transfer; and the work of the Leipzig mission and the later work of the bordering Swedish mission saved that which was about to be lost. An indigenous church was formed that stands today, strong under its own government, in India.

CHAPTER TWELVE

THE MORAVIAN MISSION

The Moravians, a pre-Reformation group, had protested against the practices of the Catholic Church. They had been persecuted and driven from place to place. The Bohemians who followed John Huss joined some Waldensians and Moravians to form the *Unitas Fratrum*. This united group sought refuge in various places, finally finding a permanent home at the estate of Count von Zinzendorf in 1722. They became one of the strongest mission groups in history.

Zinzendorf was a Lutheran, brought up in the pietist atmosphere of Halle. He became convinced that he should give up his positions with the state and give his whole life to work within the kingdom of God. He and his wife adopted the slogan, "I have one passion; it is he and he alone." He enjoyed the fellowship of the Moravians on his estate, and the settlement they formed was called *Herrnhut*. He served as advisor and counselor to these brethren for a time while still carrying out his public duties. When he resigned from his government positions, he spent all his time with them, was elected spiritual superintendent of the settlement in 1727 and was ordained as their bishop in 1737. He remained a Lutheran but sought to establish spiritually-minded groups on the Herrnhut pattern, in congregations in Europe and England.

Mission interest had come to Zinzendorf through various contacts:

Letters describing the work of the mission (Danish-Halle Mission in India) were circulated in Europe and, naturally enough, reached the Lady Gersdorf and her drawing-room meetings. Long afterwards, in August 1753, Zinzendorf told a congregation of English Moravians at Fetter Lane in London how the first seed of missionary zeal was planted in him. "I know the day, the hour, the spot in Hennersdorf," he said, "it was in the Great Room; the year was 1708 or 1709; I heard items read out of the paper about the East Indies, before the regular reports were issued; and there and then the first missionary impulse arose in my soul." "And in Francke's house at Halle," the young pietist records, "I had chances every day to hear edifying reports about the spread of the kingdom of God, to speak with witnesses from foreign lands, and to see martyrs and prisoners; and all this strengthened my zeal for the cause of Christ." In 1715 Zinzendorf dined many times at Francke's table and talked with the three Halle missionaries, home on furlough from Tranquebar.[1]

In 1731 Zinzendorf was present at the coronation of Christian VI in Denmark. There he met two natives of Greenland, who had been baptized by Hans Egede, and a converted slave from the island of St. Thomas in the West Indies. He learned of the sad plight of the natives of these islands and was deeply stirred. When he returned to Herrnhut he related what he had seen and heard, and there was almost immediate response. The seed of mission zeal was sown. Several volunteered to go as "slaves of Christ" to work in the West Indies. Two were selected.

On 18 August (1732) the whole congregation gathered in Herrnhut and in a meeting of rare fervour and expectancy they sang a hundred hymns to cheer the missionaries on their way. At three o'clock in the morning of 21 August 1732, Dober and Nitschmann stepped into the carriage outside Zinzendorf's house. The count drove them the fifteen miles to Bautzen. There they knelt by the roadside. Zinzendorf drove back to Herrnhut; the other two brethren set out on foot for Copenhagen, bundles on their backs, thirty shillings in their pockets and the invincible all-embracing love of Christ in their hearts. Thus the modern world-wide missionary movement was born. By 1740, sixty-eight Moravian missionaries had been sent out; and by the time of Zinzendorf's death in 1760, no less than 226 missionaries had gone to destinations ranging from the Arctic to the tropics, from the Far East to the American midwest.[2]

The Moravian Church has always kept this vital interest in missions. At the present time, one out of every ninety-two members of the Moravian Church is a missionary, and at one time the ratio was one out of every sixty. In other large church bodies, the average percentage of missionaries is about one for every five thousand.

This movement had tremendous impact on other areas of Europe and increased mission zeal among Christians who had already been stirred by the pietist movement and by reports from individual missionaries. Ziegenbalg from India and Guetzlaff from China had traveled in several countries speaking the mission cause in the churches. The Moravian Mission gave impetus to the formation of mission societies in Germany and Scandinavia, and stimulated mission interest in England. The missionary support by this group was wholehearted, but some of its early policies and methods were not wise.

1. They believed that throughout the world there were individuals who had already been reached by the Holy Spirit and stood ready to accept the Gospel.

The aim was not to win whole nations for Christ. This was not considered possible till the "time of the Gentiles" came. There were, however, in every nation some people whose hearts had been prepared by the Holy Spirit to accept the Gospel. These people, called "firstlings," were to be sought out and left with the Savior so his work could be carried out through them. These "firstlings" did not form a congregation of elite Christians, but were a token of the great ingathering still to come when the time of the Gentiles dawned.

2. The missionaries were supposed to support themselves and were therefore taught a trade before they left the home base. Great hardship was experienced by shoemakers who were sent to countries where the inhabitants wore no shoes, and by tailors sent where a grass skirt would do. Consequently, many of them became plantation owners and, in the competition of business, had to treat their workers in the fields on much the same basis as the non-Christian Europeans exploited the natives.

There were changes in policies later. Zinzendorf agreed that a church must be founded on every mission field. The idea of the "firstling" was not conducive to the establishing of a true, indigenous church.

Some of his policies became a part of the general theology of mission. Congregations were formed, worship was established, and the sacraments of Baptism and the Lord's Supper were immediately introduced. Later, when the number of converts increased beyond his expectation, Zinzendorf stressed the idea of an indigenous church. He depended on natives working among their own people and insisted that the missionaries must know and appreciate the customs of the land. He recognized the varied aspects of different countries, and he warned that the home base could not be considered a set pattern to be duplicated in other lands.

> Because life is so manifold and inward experiences are so different he warns missionaries against "applying the Herrnhut yardstick" or "making the private experiences of two or three people the rule over against the Saviour's plan!" As God has formed and led individuals differently so also He has created the peoples each with its own special gifts and tasks. Therefore it follows that "each should stick to his own language and ways, and the workers (missionaries) must not attempt to remold other peoples according to their own pattern."[3]

3. In establishing a method for mission work, Zinzendorf studied other missions, including what he called Egede's failure in Greenland. He felt another method should have been used there.

> In a letter to a friend in England he explained what that method was, and thereby made his first contribution to the Science of Foreign Missions. In that letter we find the germ of all his later ideas. "You are not," he wrote, "to aim at the conversion of whole nations; you must simply look for seekers after the truth who, like the Ethiopian eunuch, seem ready to welcome the Gospel. Second, you must go straight to the point and tell them about the life and death of Christ. Third, you must not stand aloof from the heathen, but humble yourself, mix with them, treat them as Brethren, and pray with them and for them." To Dober himself he talked in a similar strain . . . "What is it," he asked, "that the heathen know already?" They know that there is a God (Rom. 1:19, 20) and, therefore, the man who tells them of God is simply wasting his time. What is it that they do not know? They do not know that Christ came into the world to save sinners; and therefore the missionary must always begin with the Gospel message. And how is it that missionaries have failed in the past? They have failed because, instead of preaching Christ, they have given lectures on theology."[4]

The Moravian missionaries tried to cooperate with the existing government, even though it was colonial, and urged the people to be loyal to it. They served the government by collecting taxes, taking census, and teaching farmers, and were sometimes aided by the government. When Zinzendorf visited St. Thomas he organized the island into four districts, with an overseer for each, and arranged for a system of "hourly prayer." To the slaves he gave five rules:

> First, think constantly about Jesus Christ; let Him be as present to your minds as though you saw Him on the Cross. Second, deal honestly with Martin and his colleagues, and never pretend to be holier than you are. Third, if you are expelled for misconduct, ask for grace to repent. Fourth, be true to your husbands and wives, and obedient to masters, servants and slaves. God punished the first Negroes by making them slaves, and your conversion will make you free, not from the control of your masters, but simply from your wicked habits and thoughts, and all that makes you dissatisfied with your lot. Fifthly, think kindly of all the Negroes who have not heard the Gospel.[5]

Among the Indians in America, an effort was made to establish model villages on the Herrnhut plan.

> Zeisberger built a settlement and named it Friedenshutten (Tents of Peace); and there he endeavored to organize what we should call a model village. His settlement took the form of one long street. In the middle stood the Church on one side and the missionaries' house on the other. The converts lived in twenty-nine houses and thirteen wigwams; behind each house lay a garden; behind the gardens were cornfields, and the settlement was surrounded by a palisade. The new settlement soon acquired a reputation. Instead of merely hunting and fishing, the Indians now devoted their energies to agriculture and commerce.[6]

The model village plan used in Greenland affected every aspect of a man's life.

> The Brethren organized New Herrnhut as a Moravian settlement. For this policy their chief reason was that if they could persuade the natives to live all together in one village they would have more efficient control over their moral conduct. The natives gladly responded; New Herrnhut became a flourishing settlement; and the Brethren, following Zinzendorf's example at Herrnhut, formed their converts into bands and classes, taught the children by means of a Catechism, and once a month on

"Congregation Day" gave their people full accounts of missionary work in other lands. . . . At the same time, the Brethren organized the social, industrial, and civic life of the people. . . . Old-age pensions were introduced; a system of state insurance was devised; widows and orphans were placed under the care of heads of families; and the Brethren even passed a law that all retailers of scandalous gossip should be excluded from the meetings of the baptized. . . . For this peculiar method of work the Brethren have often been both praised and blamed. The method, let us frankly admit, had both advantages and disadvantages. On the one hand, the Eskimos learned to be good Christian citizens; on the other hand, they also learned to be too dependent on the missionaries; and the consequence was that in later years they became spoiled children.[7]

The Moravian mission of this early era made a unique contribution to the church's concept of mission and its importance to all Christians. Its influence is still a force in interdenominational and international contacts and mission conferences.

CHAPTER THIRTEEN

ERA OF THE MISSION SOCIETIES

"The great missionary enterprise" that influenced the entire world came in the nineteenth century. The missionary concept became universal among Christians and, on foundations already laid, the mission program was extended into every accessible area. This is the period when mission societies among the Protestants and missionary orders among the Catholics were organized. Their work led later to missionary programs involving whole church bodies.

Prior to this century there had been a lull in mission activity. The Catholic Church had met with a series of reverses. The "Babylonian Captivity" of the church in Avignon decreased the power of the Pope and the zeal of the members. Upon the return of the Pope to Rome, there was a controversy in the church which was not fully resolved until the Renaissance. Great effort was expended on gathering ancient documents and art objects, and in beautification of the center of the church in Rome. Rationalism followed and attacked the core of missionary evangelism in both Catholic and Protestant churches. But there were scattered fires of enthusiasm for evangelizing the world, kindled in individual hearts, and work was supported by independent Protestant organizations and Catholic orders.

The Jesuits had been placed under a ban by the Catholic Church so their missionary efforts had been hampered. In 1814 the Jesuit order was reestablished by Pope Pius VII, but it never regained its former prestige. Until 1815 the orders with strong missionary purpose had worked independently and their efforts were as weak as the order itself (except when the church gave recognition and help). From that date, however, an effort was made to enlist the entire laity in carrying out and expanding the mission program. The Society for the Propagation of the Faith, organized in 1817, grew rapidly and continues to be of great significance in the monumental missionary work carried out by the Catholic Church. It was under Pope Gregory XVI (1841-1846) that the missionary program was reorganized. A new world organization was established by setting up vicariates in the nations where congregations could be united in a church body with recognition by Rome. The training of clergymen in those areas was a step toward the formation of indigenous churches.

The Roman Church still had the policy of using government agencies for the furtherance of its missionary program in areas predominantly Catholic. Special privileges were granted them in Madagascar under Catholic governors who frequently exercised anti-Protestant policies. The result was hardship and persecution for the Protestants and political favor for those who joined the Catholic Church. In the Belgian Congo strong preference and special favors were given to Catholic missionary efforts—with severe limitations on Protestant missionaries. Later, through interchurch negotiations, a more moderate position was secured.

In Latin America missionary methods changed very little during the nineteenth century, except for adjustments to meet changing political conditions. The day of conquest was over and the day of liberation from Spain and Portugal had come. This change seemed at first to be disastrous to the church. However, through the strength of its earlier impact and with ecclesiastical adroitness, Rome retained the entire continent under her spiritual aegis, though the people took over their own national governments. Some universities and other educational institutions were founded, but the balance of ecclesiastical power was held by the Spanish and Portuguese priests. The Protestant Church was slow in coming to Latin America in any strength, so Catholicism came to be recognized as the religion of the people. There was unity in the church, but the result was a state of self-satisfaction which left it generally undeveloped, and content with nominal members.

The Society for the Propagation of the Gospel, organized in England in 1701, was originally formed for the purpose of supplying Anglican missionaries and priests for the colonial churches. A clause

was later added to the constitution declaring it was also their purpose to evangelize the pagans in all English colonies. Many Germans
from the pietist movement were called to serve under British mission societies, especially in East Africa where Krapf and Rebmann
were pioneers. In West Africa, called "the graveyard of missionaries," many tombstones bear the names of early German missionaries.

The Society for Promoting Christian Knowledge was organized
in England in 1699 with the purpose of strengthening the Christian
faith of white settlers in America and spreading the faith there.
Another early mission society was the Society for the Propagation
of the Gospel in Foreign Parts, founded in 1701. The Society for
Propagating Christian Knowledge, formed in Scotland in 1709, was
for ministry among the people of the Scottish highlands and the
American Indians. These societies had a slow start but later made
outstanding contributions to the cause of missions as their fields of
labor were broadened to include more of the newly discovered
lands.

> Books written in English have frequently spoken of William
> Carey (1761-1834) as "the father of modern missions," and
> of the work that he brought into being as the first Protestant
> mission of modern times. Our earlier chapters have shown that
> this is a misunderstanding; Carey stood, and was conscious of
> standing, in a noble succession, as the heir of many pioneers
> in the past. Yet this work does represent a turning point; it
> marks the entry of the English-speaking world on a large scale
> into the missionary enterprise—and it has been the English-
> speaking world which has provided four-fifths of the non-Roman
> missionaries from the days of Carey until the present time.[1]

Mr. Carey served as a semi-trained Baptist reader at the same time
that he plied his trade as a cobbler. On May 31, 1792, he preached
a sermon to Baptist pastors, defending a mission pamphlet that he
had previously written based on Isaiah 54:2, 3, in which was
coined the slogan, "Attempt great things for God; expect great
things from God." This led to the formation of the Baptist Missionary Society which sent Carey to India as its first missionary.
He and a teacher and a printer, all men of great ability, formed what
is called the Serampore Trio and established a mission policy that
was generally accepted by other groups during the nineteenth century. This included:

A. Extensive evangelism.

B. Widespread distribution of the Bible.

C. Education in order to have a literate and effective church membership and well-trained indigenous leadership.

D. The formation of a self-governing church as soon as feasible.

E. A thorough study of the language as well as the religious and cultural background of the people among whom they labored.

Though there was opposition from some quarters, their efforts were effective and led to a permanent mission program under the Baptist Missionary Society.

The number of mission societies increased. A partial listing includes:

Baptist Missionary Society	1792
London Missionary Society	1795
Netherlands Missionary Society	1795
Church Missionary Society	1799
Church and Foreign Bible Society	1804
Board of Commissioners for Foreign Missions (U.S.)	1810
American Baptist Missionary Board	1814
German Missionary Society	1815
Basel Mission	1824
Danish Missionary Society	1821
French Evangelical Mission	1822
Swedish Missionary Society	1835
Schreuder Mission (Norway)	1839
Norwegian Mission Society	1842
Church of Sweden Mission	1874

Many American churches maintained ties with the motherland from which their members had come, and had their mission outlet through the European missions. This delayed the formation of distinct mission societies in America, but there was real mission interest.

John Eliot started work among the Indians of America in 1646, thinking they might be the "ten lost tribes of Israel." In 1749 Jonathan Edwards wrote a book about David Brainerd which revealed deep concern and the hope that the church would become involved in a missionary program. Cotton Mather (1663-1728) was much interested in and supported the work of Ziegenbalg and the Danish mission in Tranquebar, corresponding with August Hermann Francke about missions and the establishment of God's kingdom. . . . In 1717 Mather wrote a letter directly to Ziegenbalg and Plütschau in Tranquebar expressing his praise of, and full agreement with, their "Evangelical" work.[2]

In 1802 Samuel J. Mills, a farmer in Connecticut, became convinced of a call to preach the Gospel. He studied at Williams College and while there kindled mission interest among the students. Several had gathered to discuss world affairs in reference to God's plan for the universe and their share in this plan, when it began to rain, and they took refuge in a haystack. This was the famous "Haystack Prayer Meeting" at which several students dedicated their lives to foreign missions. Those present promised to pray, ponder, and plan for mission to the heathen. Students at Andover Seminary joined the group and they organized a society called "The Brethren."

> The founders of this group brought their burden before the General Association of Congregational Ministers of Massachusetts, stating that "their minds have long been impressed with the duty and importance of personally attempting a mission to the heathen . . . and that, after examining all the information which they can obtain they consider themselves as devoted to this work for life, whenever God, in his providence, shall open the way."[3]

This message from the students led to the founding of The American Board of Commissioners for Foreign Missions, an interdenominational organization. Organized in 1810, this board sent its first missionaries in 1812 and continued expanding its work to various parts of the world.

For several reasons there was also an increased interest in missions at this time in Europe. From Dr. Kenneth Scott Latourette's analysis and list of thirteen reasons, some seem especially significant.[4] Dr. Latourette states that the overall impetus was a spiritual revival that affected both the Catholic and Protestant churches. The revival in the Catholic Church came as a rebound from the radicalism of the French Revolution. Romanticism, a reaction to the eighteenth century skepticism, stimulated many to a more ardent attachment to the church. In Germany and France the Catholic Church directed special attention to the people then experiencing a period of industrial revolution. Many of the orders of the church were reinstated and rejuvenated for this work within Europe and in foreign lands. There was increased loyalty to the church and stricter observance of religious duties. The revival was even stronger among Protestant churches. Beginning with the pietist movement, there was a rekindling of active Christian life with emphasis on obedience to the Word of God and following the example of Christ. New Christian movements sprang up, especially among student groups. Mass impact was made on members of Protestant churches by men like Moody, Drummond, and John R. Mott. The World Student Christian Federation, the Young Men's Christian Association, the Young Women's Christian Association and the denominational youth groups date from this time. This was also the time for the development of new denominations. All these provided both the seed-bed and the stimulus to mission activity.

Some of the specific features of missions in this period were:

1. The absence of government assistance. In most instances the program was kept as a spiritual effort of the church.

2. The expansion of Christianity became an enterprise of the rank and file of the membership of churches. Missions, instead of being narrowed down to be the limited activity of the few, were expanded to demand the interest and support of the mass of believers.

3. An increased participation in the work by women (both in home-base support and as active workers on the mission fields) made it possible to contact many people hitherto unreached.

4. Admission to church membership on mission fields was based on faith of individuals, in contrast to the mass conversions through ecclesiastical strategy or various types of pressure. A higher standard was set for admission, resulting in a strong church though only a small minority of the country's people were members. The Christian minorities in primitive areas were forerunners of a new culture and advance. Advance in education, medicine, and other fields was usually initiated by the missions and brought enlightenment that people respected and wanted.

5. Peaceful conditions gave opportunity for uninterrupted mission work in most areas of the world.

6. A new world culture was developing under Western leadership that made impact on non-European cultures. This opened the world to influences from the West. The emergence of English as a world language made communication easier.

It is in times of sociological change that man is most open to new ideas. This was a century of many changes, some of which contributed directly, others indirectly, to the advance of missions. In missions history, this period has been called "The Great Century."

Special consideration should be given to the relationship of mission societies to the church, and to the pattern set for mission work during this period.

Each mission society had its individual development, so a general analysis will not apply equally well to all. Generally the societies, drawing support for their work from members within the churches, were unhindered and, in some instances, encouraged by church officials. The societies were active in interesting people to participate in their particular missions, and often appealed to the people who had been influenced by the pietist movement or spiritual awakenings.

Mission zeal was rooted in these movements. The interest of these people was for "a living faith" in the church and active mission work abroad. They were a nucleus serving as a leavening medium among other church members, where possible. Their intense zeal contrasted with the lukewarmness or indifference often characteristic of church-supported missions. The very fact that people became busy in a society had the tendency to set them apart, and much of their witness and Christian experience was found within the society. If regular services were held in separate society halls, the church as a whole was robbed of participation in mission work. Where both church and society had mutual fellowship and interest in missions, this breach was avoided, and the church was frequently able to exercise its mission interest through a congenial society.

It was difficult for a state church, as an official branch of the government, to engage in direct mission work. A state-church mission could immediately be looked upon as the arm of a government seeking control of a foreign land. Cooperation of the church with a mission society was a way of avoiding the risk of such accusations. Where the mission society was formed because of lack of interest within the church for missions, such action was actually a judgment on the church. A separate organization resulted—not because of doctrinal differences, but because of different emphases in Christian life and practice.

There was a definite pattern for mission work generally followed at this time.

1. All societies worked toward the ideal of forming self-supporting, indigenous congregations.

2. In most cases the societies gave the missionaries salaries. Only a few required the missionary to support himself by plying his trade as he preached the Gospel. Schools, hospitals, training centers, and other necessary institutions were established by the societies in order to prepare the people for leadership in the indigenous church. The cost of operating these institutions, though small according to Western standards, was a burden that the young church could not assume because of the standards of living and economy.

3. The mission compound developed. In India it was difficult for Christian converts to retain their faith against the assaults of the caste and family. The missionary thought it wise to place them in a Christian atmosphere where they could be thoroughly trained in the faith to become effective evangelists among their own people. The missionary residence became the hub around which residences of Christians, schools, and other institutions were built. In some places in Africa, native Christians moved to the neighborhood of the missionary to have the security of his presence and access to schools provided for his children and to other facilities found at the mission station. In the sparsely settled bush country, this was natural, but from it something akin to the "compound" developed. This "compound pattern" was followed into the twentieth century. What was a natural development in that age is now recognized to have had shortcomings in that it hampered the spread of the Gospel by forming cells of Christianity rather than letting it be the salt in the whole society. The formation of the indigenous church was delayed.

4. A strong, Bible-centered program of evangelism was wholesome and was geared to the understanding of the people.

5. Education for the enlightenment of the people, and also more

specifically for the training of native leadership in evangelism and education, was stressed.

6. Both translated and original Christian literature was produced. In many countries the language of the people had to be reduced to writing before literacy could be achieved and literature produced. This was done by the missionaries, who proceeded immediately to provide literature that would introduce Christ and would strengthen the faith of the new Christians.

7. Ecumenical consciousness was more strong and deep on the mission fields than in the homelands. A Christian moving from one place to another was usually recognized as a brother in the faith, even though the mission in the new area might be of a different denomination. Fellowship among missionaries of many denominations was natural. Where Christians are a weak minority, the fact of being Christian immediately binds men together in a brotherhood that respects the other's faith in a common Lord. Realization that the mission task is too large for any single society or denomination led to official cooperation through what is known as the "Comity Agreement." A voluntary system of establishing particular mission fields for the various denominations and societies was set up whereby boundaries of one mission were respected by the other. In this way local competition between denominations was avoided, and respect for the work of other Christian agencies was engendered.

One of the weaknesses of this period was the individualism that developed in each of the many mission societies and agencies not directly connected with a church body. They were forced to make their own policies. It was unfortunate but it was natural that their own particular emphases and practices from the homeland became the pattern for procedure on the mission fields. With many societies, there were naturally many policies, many hymnbooks, many liturgical forms. It is inevitable that a missionary is influenced by his past heritage in his method of proclaiming the Gospel. Difficulty arises when past traditions and rigid forms of worship are transplanted in so many varying forms that confusion results.

CHAPTER FOURTEEN

RELATION OF CHURCH
TO MISSION

In the latter half of the nineteenth century the churches began to take greater interest and assume more support for missions. There was, therefore, a partial transfer of responsibility for the mission program from the society to the church.

In the *Landeskirchen* and the formally organized state churches of Europe, a vigorous official mission program would have been both embarrassing and difficult. Any mission effort outside their own colonies might have been interpreted as aggressive acts of the state. In most instances nationalistic feeling kept them within the bounds of their own nations and colonies. Mission interest among church leaders and lay people was usually absorbed by the flourishing mission societies. The Church Missionary Society (England), the Church of Sweden Mission, and the Norwegian Mission Society received hearty support from church members and semi-official recognition from their state churches. Many societies, however, carried out their work with no recognition or support from the official church.

When the American Board of Commissioners for Foreign Missions was formed in 1810, it was patterned after the European societies. It was not long before complications arose within this Board. Several denominations were represented in the organization and, as mission interest increased in America, the various denominations felt the urge to start their own independent work. This marked the beginning of the shift from society to church as the responsible mission agency. It became the general pattern of mission organization within the United States and Canada. In recent years, with the gradual dissolution of colonial empires and the changed relation between church and state in some countries, mission executives in Europe have considered the advisability of changing their plan so that the relationship would be directly from European church to mission church, rather than from society to mission church. The first definite step in this direction was taken about 1960, when Bishop Heinrich Meyer of Lübeck inspired his people to take direct responsibility as a church to support a mission already in existence.

Mission societies depend on the intensive interest of the few, but support of missions has not been limited to the few. In state churches, salaries of the clergy, property acquisition, and upkeep and other expenses for local congregations are paid from tax revenues. The only outlet for voluntary giving by Christians, in many instances, has been through the inner mission and world mission programs. The general membership of the church has contributed funds for this work, though the direct responsibility remained with the society.

In America the total program of the church, at home and abroad, is the responsibility of every member. The intensity of interest and generous support of some members of smaller mission societies is difficult to attain in the church missions, but there too there are individuals and groups that manifest their special interest with generous gifts. The work of mission requires the spiritual and material resources of the entire church if the demands and possibilities of our day are to be met.

Both the societies and the churches engaged in mission work sought to build indigenous churches on the mission fields. In the early work of the Danish-Halle Mission under Ziegenbalg and the Baptist Mission Society under Carey, well-defined action was taken to carry out this policy.

Henry Venn, secretary of the Church Missionary Society of London (from 1841), and his good friend Rufus Anderson, secretary of the Commission for Foreign Missions for the Congregationalists in America, were some of the earliest spokesmen for this principle.

As early as 1854, Henry Venn, the prescient Secretary of the Church Missionary Society in London, had spoken in terms of the aim of mission as being the calling into existence of self-governing, self-supporting, and self-propagating Churches; and of the euthanasia of a mission. Once the mission has brought a Church into being, it may die out in that area; the missionaries may go on to the unevangelized regions, and leave the Church which they had brought into being to fulfill, under the guidance of the Holy Spirit, all the functions of the Church.[1]

Venn approached the problem of the indigenous church on the basis of the Anglican church structure, envisioning dioceses linking congregations on the mission field together, and they in turn in some relationship with the church in England.

Rufus Anderson was equally ardent for the establishment of an indigenous church, but as a Congregationalist he saw it organized on the basis of the individual congregations. The churches he envisioned were easier to attain. In order to maintain their organizational simplicity he discouraged the expansion of education programs lest they become larger than the churches they were to serve. He saw the need for having missionaries supervise the congregations for a while, as Paul supervised churches established in his time. These congregations were to be evangelistic forces for the total mission program, working together with the missionaries in fellowship under the divine missionary compulsion.

> Anderson's main emphasis . . . is on mission, not on church organization. This is seen in the priorities indicated by his description of the Church as, first, self-propagating; secondly, self-governing; and thirdly, self-supporting. . . . It is in the context of his passionate desire to evangelize that we are to understand his belief that mission churches ought to be rendered autonomous. For Venn the constitution of autonomous churches means setting the missionary free for his own proper evangelistic task. For Anderson, on the other hand, the young local churches themselves are means towards the evangelistic end. "Missions," he says in his *Outlines of Missionary Policy*, as early as 1856, "are instituted for the spread of a scriptural, self-propagating Christianity. This is their only aim."[2]

These principles were generally accepted by all missionary organizations, but in practice they varied greatly. In some areas missionaries were withdrawn so early that the young churches suffered and were dissolved, not having been firmly enough rooted to withstand the constant pressure of their pagan societies. In other places, a spirit of paternalism developed that restrained the missions from granting self-government and delayed the development of indigenous churches. There has been much study and much discussion of these principles within mission circles in later years as the pressure for independence has increased.

One of the earliest missionaries to put these principles into practice was Karl Gützlaff, who arrived in China in 1831. After several trips along the coast, he became a missionary with permanent residences in Macao and Hong Kong. He made many trips into the interior and along the coast, and was active until his death (1851) interpreting China to the people of Europe and America, seeking to stimulate their mission interest. Travel was dangerous and at times forbidden during his years in China, and contact with the interior was difficult. Effective evangelistic work was conducted in Macao, Hong Kong, and Canton, and some of the Christians from these cities were trained to be evangelists. Gützlaff prepared Christian literature in Chinese, including a new translation of the Bible, books of religious and cultural content, tracts, and periodicals. The evangelists who had been trained served as colporteurs of this literature in hopes that it might prepare the people of China to accept the Word of God. Gützlaff hoped the Gospel would soon be preached widely throughout the country by an army of missionaries from America and Europe. When he finally was forced to realize that this army of missionaries was not forthcoming, he formulated a new policy. He had been impressed by the value of Chinese co-workers in his many efforts of evangelism and concluded that the work of Christianizing China was not dependent on foreign missionaries. He became assured that it would be accomplished by Chinese Christians. His experience with two of his Chinese co-workers, Chang and Jio, encouraged him.

There were further travels in 1839. Chang reported he had visited the borders of Kiangsu and had established two schools. Jio worked along the border of Fukien. Gützlaff said that he had other persons who were qualified to be sent out in addition to them. It was, however, in the beginning of 1840 that he began seriously to count on native co-workers to accomplish the work. In the March first issue of *Nederlandsch Zendelinggenottschap* he wrote that he found it necessary to train a number of native Christians as evangelists who were to travel in the interior of China. He requested financial support for five or six such evangelists.[3]

This was just the beginning. He must certainly have been aware that five or six evangelists would be insufficient to evangelize China. By 1841 he had trained and commissioned twenty, and reports indicate that a few years later there were over eighty such evangelists at work. The plan was that each of them, with a supply of books and tracts, would push into the interior of China where he was to use every possible opportunity to proclaim the Gospel. Propelled by his own zeal for the evangelization of his countrymen, he was to use his own initiative in adapting method to opportunity. Reports were to be given to Gützlaff following such trips by each evangelist. These reports were usually very encouraging.

Gützlaff recognized the risk involved in this method of evangelism, knowing that some who were sent out might be dishonest in their reports and insincere in their profession of faith. It was not long before he had to answer some rather pointed questions raised by fellow missionaries and members of the home board, who doubted the validity of the method. But Gützlaff continued and expanded the program with his undying optimism and his faith that the Holy Spirit would accomplish the work even through imperfect witnesses. To give greater stability to the work and to make it indigenous in all aspects, Gützlaff organized the Chinese co-workers into a "Missionary Association." Evangelists, and all who had been brought to faith in Christ through them, were listed as members. Hymnbooks and a prayer book for regular services were provided.

> Something of the program of the organization is indicated in the name "Chinese" association. It implied that it was the Chinese themselves who had the aim of spreading the Gospel in their own country and had joined together for this purpose. In the letter giving the reasons for formation of the association . . . it was mentioned, "We are, therefore, united as brothers at the foot of the cross to glorify God in China, our native land, with singleness of heart and hand."[4]

Gützlaff was the leader of this association, but responsibility and control were to be vested in the Chinese Christians. Every effort was made to put the principle of a truly indigenous church into action. There was, however, a gap between principle and practice. Some missionaries came out from Germany and it was not long before they saw the weakness in the program.

Those sent from Germany to aid him early suspected that many
of his Chinese helpers were not really Christian, and while he
was in Germany, Hamberg, who had been left in charge in
Hongkong, discovered that he had been thoroughly deceived.
. . . Little if any travelling had been done outside Hongkong and
the vicinity, and only a small minority of helpers were honest.
On his return Gützlaff was confronted with the disheartening
facts and planned a more adequate supervision by Europeans.
He did not live to retrieve his mistake, however, but died in
1851.[5]

The work that Gützlaff had started was continued by his German
brethren who made a few changes in policy, but the concept of the
indigenous church was not forgotten, nor was it lost sight of in
other missionary endeavors. Many of the early efforts made at establishing such churches were theoretically commendable but prac-
tically unattainable. Efforts to first build a strong church foundation, under a mission, with the understanding that the church would
later become independent, sometimes proved successful; but often
it floundered where the mission and the church became accustomed
to a mission-directed program, and plain inertia hindered the development of the church. It has been necessary to have periods
when policy and development of missions could be examined and
evaluated in light of the ultimate goal—the formation of indigenous
churches in every land.

The twentieth century has been such a time of reexamination of
missions. Criticism of missionary work has come from outside the
church and from within; from sympathetic supporters and from
individuals who have not seen the importance of the enterprise and
have approached it in a spirit of hostility; from those who sought to
increase its effectiveness and from those who would minimize its
importance, seek to discredit it, and have it discontinued. Criticism
has also come from missionaries and students of missions, for there
is no group of workers in the kingdom of God so ready to be examined and to accept constructive criticism as those in charge of missions, both on the field and at home base.

This spirit of self-examination has led to great international missionary conferences which have produced many volumes on the
theory and practice of mission. The first of the great missionary
conferences was held in Edinburgh in 1910. At that time the missionary expansion into new lands, new areas, and new activities

was phenomenal. The dominance of Western powers was felt within the world in its colonial control and general influence. As a result other nations were open to Western influence. Christianity confronted the people of Africa and Asia with the prestige of the West and with an inner spirit of evangelism that was outstandingly dynamic. On the other hand, the pagan faiths were generally in a state of decadence and dormancy, leaving an open door for the propagation of the Christian Gospel.

The people who met in Edinburgh were ready for missionary advance. There was a spirit of optimism, a looking forward to the time when all the world would know Christ. The urgency of the hour was stressed both from the viewpoint of the open doors and Christian eschatology. The keynote was: "This is the decisive hour for the evangelization of the world." Dr. John R. Mott in the closing address said,

> The end of the conference is the beginning of the conquest. . . .
> He is summoning us to larger sacrifice, one that is like unto a
> new experience, like unto a revolution, a transformation. Our
> best days are ahead of us . . . there is the need not only of reality
> but the need of immediacy. The sense of urgency should stride
> into the core of each one of us—even the most obscure dele-
> gate.[6]

This was the day of the Student Volunteer Movement with its slogan: "The evangelization of the world in this generation." There was something tremendously overpowering and inspiring in the approach of the conference that cleared the air of many misconceptions and differences between the missionizing agencies and brought a spiritual unity in the program throughout the world. Dr. A. Lehman has called it "the birth place of that international and interdenominational Christian co-operation which is characteristic of our country."[7]

This conference was a stock-taking by the missionary sending bodies and a comparison of notes by missionaries. It was in every aspect a *missionary* conference. Only seventeen of the 1,300 to 1,400 delegates were from the churches established on the mission fields. Even they came as representatives of the sending bodies and not of their own churches. There has been criticism of this conference for the above reason. It was undoubtedly true that it was missionary-centered and did not come to grips with the relationship

between mission and church. There was a consciousness of the
church, but it was perhaps considered, not as an entity already in
existence, but as a "fruit of missions." It is possible that the great
missionary leaders of that day followed intuitively the impelling
force of missions somewhat as the apostles did following Pentecost.
They did not first sit down to laboriously study motivation and policy for the purpose of establishing a theology of mission *before*
they went out to preach Christ. They knew the need of the world.
They knew that the saving message of Christ could meet that need.
They felt the urgency of the time between Christ's first coming and
his return to the earth, and they were impelled to proclaim the
message of salvation, the Holy Spirit working with them to accomplish the God-given mission.

The second great international missionary conference was held in
Jerusalem in 1928. This conference met in times that were quite
different from 1910. The first World War had been fought. With
the new spirit of independence and aspiration in every nation of
the world, there was also a new sense of man's need for self-ex-
pression, and consequently of self-determination on the part of the
younger churches. The church had emerged. There was a new self-
consciousness on the part of the representatives of churches from
Africa, the Orient, and the islands of the two seas, calling for recognition of them by the churches of the West. In this conference the
question of "mission and church" and "church and church" (older
and younger) came to the forefront. More than one-fifth of the
delegates to this assembly were from the "younger churches." They
participated officially as representatives of a missionary society.
Some of the delegates from the Orient took a leading part in the
discussions and in determining the findings. The question of the
validity of the missionary message was raised. Were not all religions
equally valid? Could not the writings of Buddhism and Hinduism
serve as "Old Testaments" of the churches located in countries
where those religions prevail? Was there not a gradual growth
from the one religion to the other? The conclusion drawn was that
Christ is *the way* of salvation. There was not, however, a clear-cut
agreement by all as to whether Christianity was *sui generis* or simply
unique in some special way. The total uniqueness of Christianity
was recognized in the statement adopted by the council.

In this world, bewildered and groping for its way, Jesus Christ has drawn to Himself the attention and admiration of mankind as never before. He stands before men as plainly greater than Western civilization, greater than the Christianity that the world has come to know. Many who have not hitherto been won to His Church yet find in Him their hero and their ideal. Within His Church there is a widespread desire for the unity centered in His Person.

Against this background and in relation to it, we have to proclaim our message.

Our message is Jesus Christ. He is the revelation of what God is and of what man through Him may become. In Him we come face to face with the Ultimate Reality of the universe; He makes known to us God as our Father, perfect and infinite in love and in righteousness; for in Him we find God incarnate, the final, yet ever-unfolding, revelation of the God in whom we live and move and have our being.[8]

The statement was further strengthened by referring to the Lausanne declaration of the World Conference on Faith and Order, accepted in 1927. The statement was clear, but it was evident from the discussions that there were various interpretations of it.

Great emphasis was placed on the Christian life. There was an attempt by some speakers to effect a theological synthesis between Christianity and the various religions of the nations. No doubt, in some of the sessions, the spirit of nationalism or humanism of the age was evident. The final words of the findings have been interpreted in different ways by different people. At the close of the conference Christianity was spoken of as an influence for bettering countries of the world. This statement might indicate that the goal of missions is Christian ethics rather than conversion to Christ; and a "Christianized" world rather than a new heaven and new earth.

Before and after the Jerusalem conference many books were written on the theory and practice of mission. William Hocking wrote *Rethinking Missions*. In discussing the book, we who were missionaries in China at the time agreed that none of us had the qualifications for being a missionary, according to Hocking, but we knew that we *did* have the message. (A skit presented by the missionaries one summer at Kuling was based on Hocking's book. A board of missionary experts sat in judgment on a young missionary candidate who came bouncing into the room with enthusiasm, ready to go at a moment's notice to any place in the world where they would send him. But he had only a college degree and seminary diploma. He must specialize. After six years of additional study, he appeared again before the board only to be told that there were still some gaps in his preparation for being an effective missionary. When he finally came before the board with all necessary academic requirements, he was a toddling old man with gray beard, trembling hands, and cane to steady his steps—too old to go.) Hocking's book was one of the more extremely critical presentations of that period.

The question of the uniqueness and supremacy of Christianity as the reason for the existence of mission was discussed anew. Ernst Troeltsch claimed that Christianity is valid for us, but that other religions might be valid for other people as long as they remain as they are culturally. In other words, Christianity and all religions are relatively dependent on the cultural advances of the people. He insisted that Christianity, whether regarded as a whole or in its several forms, "is purely a historical, relative phenomenon, which could . . . only have arisen in the territory of the classical culture, and among the Latin and German races. . . . It stands or falls with European civilization."[9]

The sociologists who were prone to look at religion as a part of the cultural development of man spoke of religious change as being a distinction between primary and secondary societal forms. Primary forms, concerned with self-preservation mores, and secondary forms, concerned with self-perpetuation mores, were thought to be the factors governing religion. Religion was not considered to be based on divine revelation. According to this view mission was to be concerned primarily with man's cultural development, providing a cross-fertilization of the cultures of the world.

Dr. William Hocking, in his definition of religion as "man's hold on what is eternal and true for all men" or "a passion for righteousness, and for the spread of righteousness, conceived as a cosmic demand," spoke of a world culture emerging and wondered if a world religion is not necessary as a complement to this new culture. He spoke of synthesis of "truths" found in the various religions. The selection is to be made, not by comparison or analysis, but by induction, "namely a perception for the reason why a given group of facts or experiences belong together."[10] Dr. Hocking, assured in his own mind of the uniqueness of Christianity and that there could not be a world faith without it, interpreted the spirit of the age to demand that if there were to be a religion it would be a world religion. Present religions were considered to be mere "localisms," and therefore unessential. The age looked on them as outmoded subjectivisms exuding only the stale air of the past, a sharp contrast with the freshness of the "world religion" still to be defined. The implication was that Buddha, Jesus, and Mohammed would be dismissed with thanks for the past and left in their private little closets as important relics. Religion is recognized as being a product of cultures of certain ages and societal backgrounds, or subjective conclusions drawn by religious leaders within these various changing cultures. Truth is therefore relative to a particular culture, and is dependent on its usefulness to society at a particular time.

The epitome of this criticism of missions is given in an article written during this period of rationalism:

> I simply do not hold the view expressed by Dr. John R. Mott, in his "Decisive Hour for Christian Missions"—and still, I suppose, the view held by the great majority of sponsors of the missionary enterprise is—"that Christianity . . . is the only religion for all mankind." I believe that there are other religions which will meet the needs of other men, just as there are other cultures and other forms of government than ours that will meet their needs. I have no more desire to Christianize the world than I have to Americanize it. Both seem to me to contain elements of imperialistic desire to dominate and egoistic desire to cast all lives into our mould which are contrary to the truly Christian spirit. The kind of missionary enterprise which I should like to see promoted is one which seeks the cooperation of all men of good will, regardless of religion, color, or race, for the enrichment and liberation of human life and the building of a better world. . . . We should welcome the people of other religions if they come, but . . . we should not be too greatly surprised if some Christians come to see other religious interpretations of experience as more satisfying than that to which they have been accustomed.[11]

During this time, anyone confessing a faith of assurance in Christ was accused of spiritual arrogance, for Christianity was reduced to the level of the religions of the world that were *seeking* for truth. The thought of "proclaiming the Gospel" became distasteful, and man adopted the new catch-phrase, "partners in a common quest." Oscar MacMillan Buck, seeking to find the uniqueness of Christianity over other religions, declared that it lay in the concept of "the fatherhood of God."

> The second perfection, of course, comes axiomatically out of the first. If there is a Fatherly rule of God, then human society must eventually correspond to it, must progressively and in increasingly large units approximate it—its derived perfection matching the originating purpose. The second perfection comes out of "the Father's good pleasure" to give us the kingdom.[12]

Albert Schweitzer had confidence in an ability to reach truth by man's individual elemental thinking based on "reverence for life." According to him the function of missions was: (1) to build a civilization upon the foundation of agriculture and handicraft, (2) to alleviate and correct the ills of Western exploitation, and (3) to make atonement for the suffering the white people have caused. All these are to be carried out in the ethical spirit that flows from the recognition that all people are a brotherhood, a "brotherhood of those who bear the mark of pain."[13]

The Jerusalem discussions concerning the validity of Christianity and its uniqueness did not end in a satisfactory conclusion. Since those contributing to the discussion went in different directions from varying premises, no unified solution could be reached. The two main problems left open for discussion at a future conference were (1) the relationship of Christianity to the religions of the world, and (2) the nature of the church. The International Mission Conference of 1938, held in Madras, India, was very church-centric in its approach to the problems facing missions. The five main themes of the conference were related to the church:

1. The Faith by which the Church Lives

2. The Witness of the Church

3. The Life of the Church

4. The Church in Its Environment

5. Cooperation and the Unity of the Church

The premise and the conclusion of the conference was: "That mission and church are indissolubly related to one another."

The book issued as a preparatory study for the conference was *The Christian Message in a Non-Christian World* by Hendrik Kraemer. He discounted some of the suggestions made at the Jerusalem Conference: that there was a general contribution of non-Christian religions to the Christian faith, that there was an evolution of lower forms of religion to the higher, and that followers of ethnic religions, through their non-Christian tenets, might, through their earnest zeal, achieve all that a Christian receives through his faith. Although the Jerusalem Conference had ended with the statement that Christ is the only message we have to give, the questions raised earlier had never been settled. Kraemer met them with the statement of "discontinuity"—that Christianity and all other religions are entities in their own totalities and that there is not continuous progress from the one into the other. He wrote:

> Somehow the conviction is alive that it is possible and feasible to produce for every religion a sort of catalogue of points of contact. This apparently is a misguided pursuit . . . religion is nowhere in the world an assortment of spiritual commodities, that can be compared as shoes or neckties. . . . Every religion is an indivisible, and not to be divided, unity of existential apprehension.[14]

In one of the opening messages of the conference, Dr. Kraemer stated:

> The Christian revelation, as the record of God's self-disclosing revelation in Jesus Christ, is absolutely *sui generis*. It is the story of God's sovereign redeeming acts having become decisively and finally manifest in Jesus Christ, the Son of the Living God, in Whom God became flesh and revealed His grace and truth.[15]

> Christianity in the dynamic sense of the word is not a set of sublime religious and moral ideas and ideals, nor is it a body of circumscribed truths which bind a man's mind, but it is the divinely wrought objective reality of a newly established relation between God and man in which is opened up the possibility of a life of real fellowship with God. To proclaim the Gospel means to entreat men, in God's name, to participate in this reality. In the first Epistle of Peter this is expressed in words ringing with the joy of salvation: "Blessed be the God and Father of our Lord Jesus Christ. By his great mercy we have been born anew to a life of hope through the resurrection of Jesus Christ from the dead."[16]

With the church as the center (the term "church" taken in the the meaning and context of European theological thinking) there was a solid foundation. After the conference was over, however, it was evident that there had been some confusion as to what the term "church" actually meant. This had not been cleared up during the conference, so there was continued identification of "church" with "sending agency" (mission society or denomination) by some, and with "receiving body" (younger church) on the mission field by others. "Church" as originally presented to the conference referred to the fellowship of believers throughout the world—"the communion of saints"—the union in Christ of all believers, under the Holy Spirit. In this sense, the idea that "the church is mission" can be understood. In other words, the church is God's agency for carrying out his plan of salvation for the world. Naturally the organized church in its denominational or segmented geographical settings can never be equated with God's great missionary program.

> We spoke no more of eastern and western churches, no more of missions and churches; we spoke of the Church, the community of God in the world and of its all-important task, in which the older and the younger churches, the sending churches and the churches that are coming into being, participate on absolutely equal terms. The sanctuary of God is being built among the peoples, and black hands and white, brown hands and yellow are engaged in the task.[17]

The definition of "church" that was used in the conference was no doubt correct. At the same time this "church" was spoken of in many terms—"older," "younger," "sending," "receiving," "coming into being," etc. Their relationships to each other and to the common task were not fully dealt with, in the effort to show the *oneness* of the church in Christ. Involved are at least three organizations, each a part of *the church*. (1) The church body in Europe or America supporting a mission. (2) The mission. (3) The church established in mission areas. Clarification of the relationships from church to mission to church, or just from mission to church, or just from church to church, was left to the future.

Much was accomplished at the Madras Conference, however. The establishing of the concept of the oneness of the church was a very important, significant contribution to future discussions concerning the various divisions within the church.

The delegates to the conference sought to interpret the changing world situation as it affected the message and program of missions and the function of the missionary. Marked developments took place between the Jerusalem and Madras conferences. A new sense of the value and dignity of the individual had developed in every area of the world. This was especially true in African and Asian countries where people had previously been forced by circumstances into situations that engendered feelings of inferiority and uncertainty. In some areas, this development manifested itself in a new sense of equality among all Christians in Christ and partnership in the responsibility of proclaiming the Gospel. In other places it led to an intense spirit of nationalism which manifested itself in anti-Western attitudes. In all countries, the indigenization of the churches had developed rapidly in depth as well as in external organization. Madras was truly a conference of the churches of the world, younger and older, meeting to face unanswered problems, to direct procedure in meeting new situations, and to plan for the future—not as "brothers in a common quest," but as a fellowship within the church that had the message needed by the world in all ages.

At the World Mission Conference at Willingen in 1952 the theological nature of the church and its relationship to mission was discussed under the theme: "The Missionary Obligation of the Church." The findings of the conference were not conclusive. Two statements of the theological committee were adopted: "A statement of the missionary calling of the church" and "A statement on the calling of the church to mission and unity." No unanimity was reached on the theological study of the nature of the church and its relationship to mission. Willingen made important contributions toward a theology of mission for the church, but did not come with the final answers. The theme of the conference was not well chosen. Mission is greater than an "obligation of the church." The discussions led beyond the church as an organization in this world, to the eternal mission plan of God and the history of salvation through God's acts as recorded in the Old and New Testaments, and through his continuing acts in history until his purpose for man is fulfilled.

> If we wish to discover anew the theological basis of the missionary enterprise, if it is our purpose to formulate a theology of missions, it is not the Church which should be the starting-

point of our investigation, and our thought must not remain confined within the boundaries and limits of the Church. Theologically, we must dig deeper, we must trace out the originating impulse in faith in the triune God, from that standpoint alone can we see the missionary enterprise synoptically in its relationship to the Kingdom of God and its relationship to the world.[18]

The theme developed at Willingen in embryo is now being given form in various publications. The topics in these books and pamphlets are numerous: "The relation between history and the history of salvation"; "Mission and eschatology"; "The nature of the church and the Christian ministry"; "The theological distinction between foreign mission and mission responsibility in general"; "The relationship between American and European churches and churches that have been established in mission lands"; and so on.

The general trend of the discussion carried out in post-Willingen years is suggested in the title of Dr. Leslie Newbigin's book *Trinitarian Faith and Today's Mission.* There is a deep implication in this title that mission is not initiated by the church, but is the act of God the Father, through redemption in Jesus Christ, by the agency of the Holy Spirit. No chronological order is indicated, but God the Father, God the Son, and God the Holy Spirit are all involved in the story of salvation and its proclamation in the past and in the now. Dr. Newbigin lays stress on prevenient grace as the work of the Spirit, and the work of the Spirit is through the church. Dr. Andersen, in his book *Toward a Theology of Mission,* also implies that the work of the Spirit is through the church. Dr. Max Warren quotes a statement by Dr. Freytag which points to the very fact of the existence of churches as God's act of mission.

Perhaps the theological dimension, as Professor Freytag sees it, can best be described in two quotations from a recent paper of his entitled "The Historical Setting of Missions." "Our missionary task is only a part of the Mission of the Church. Because we again and again apply the biblical message on the missionary task to our human undertakings, we are not aware of the fact that the Bible speaks about God's Mission and the role of the Church in it not only in the form of the command 'I send you,' but also in an entirely different way which has nothing to do with human undertakings. The great promises of the Old Testament which prophesy the gathering together of the heathen on Mount Zion, as Isaiah XXV, 6-9,

Zechariah VIII, 21, and many more had nothing to do with missionary undertakings. This line of God's promises continues in the New Testament with the metaphor of the city set on a hill and the light on a stand and others. There the Bible speaks about the Church as the Mission in that sense that living churches by their very existence are acts of God towards His goal with the world. As a matter of course, there is no Christian life in the biblical sense of the word, which is not aware of being a part of this action of God towards the world. But what happens there is not in the line of human undertakings. It is part of the mystery of the eschatological existence of the Church . . . . What happens there is Mission as God's action."[19]

The presentations differ because there are different theological concepts. Without discounting the role of the church in mission, each seeks to lift the Christian's vision beyond the church to God for the ultimate fulfillment of the mission objective. There is an emphasis on the lordship of God, not only over the church, but over all the world and all history. This thought is tied in with God's self-revelation through the history of salvation *(Heilsgeschichte)* which is manifest in the past and which he still directs.

There is a dual implication for the church that is of great importance. The church must realize that mission is *God's* work and the church can, therefore, at best be an instrument in God's hand. If it becomes anything less than this, the program will fail, however scientifically correct its methods and manner of approach may be. On the other hand, mission, as God's work, cannot fail. Missions have had phenomenal successes in the past in spite of weaknesses. Changes, opposition, problems arising in the world, which seem to seriously affect mission, are not so alarming as they seem at first sight. God will carry his program through to its ultimate conclusion. The church can, therefore, continue in assurance that God, who directs his plan, will give the church needed wisdom for each hour. The church's concern is that it be obedient to God and open to the guidance of the Holy Spirit.

The discussions continued. Even in the post-Willingen period it is difficult to find a meeting of minds because of varied theological backgrounds. Dr. Andersen has pointed out the differences that appeared at Madras. It was agreed that to find the starting point for a theology of mission one would have to go deeper than the Willingen theme, "The Missionary Obligation of the Church." The

American Reformed view seemed to be that the starting point should not be the church, but Jesus Christ's proclamation of the kingdom of God. The Anglicans maintained that the witness to the incarnation of the Son of God is the starting point for the extension of the church. The Europeans and American Lutherans emphasized that the cross—with the forgiveness of sins in Christ, new life of discipleship in Christ and justification of the sinner through faith alone—must be the starting point.

There were other problems. It was agreed that God does work in history but that it is difficult to determine what is God's work and what is revolution against God, or simply self-assertiveness on the part of individual church leaders. The trinitarian work in missions was considered self-evident, but the specific work of the Holy Spirit in relation to the church was left an open question. Would the Holy Spirit work through the existing church or through a church altered to meet the changing circumstances in the world? The relationship of mission to the political powers within the world was also discussed. The central question upon which the others hinged, was the question of the church in relation to mission. Dr. Andersen points up the general trend of the discussions:

> The Church is not the true center of gravity towards which missionary thinking should be directed. In a theology of the missionary enterprise we have to turn back to the self-revelation of the Triune God in Jesus Christ; only so can we discover the true and final principles which we seek.[20]

> To accept the Cross as the only possible starting-point for a theology of mission is to escape the danger of seeking a speculative basis for the theology. The Cross stands at the centre of human history, and calls us to take history seriously. (Freytag: *Mission zwischen Gerstern und Morgen;* p. 49). If we seek to find the source of the missionary enterprise in the triune God, we must take our stand on the acts which God has wrought in History—otherwise we follow arbitrarily our own fancies. The Cross is not a timeless symbol; it is the sign of Jesus Christ, through whose death and resurrection God had decisively taken a hand in human history. It does not directly answer the questions of the world, since those are not the questions that need to be asked. "It confronts the world with the real questions, which are God's questions—casting down all that exalts itself in defiance of Him, bringing to nothing the idolatries by which men are deceived." But it reveals God not

only as the Judge but also as the Savior, since it raised "up those who are sunk in disillusionment and despair" (*Missions Under the Cross,* p. 188).[21]

The witness of the Cross is twofold: God in Christ has brought in His sovereign rule; therefore it is His will that this Gospel of the Kingdom should be preached to all the nations upon earth for a witness unto them; but parallel with this is the other truth—the battle is still engaged between His hidden Kingdom and the opposing spiritual powers. There is no room for neutrality in this conflict. Every man must choose this day whom he will serve.[22]

CHAPTER FIFTEEN

MISSION PROBLEMS OF OUR AGE

The geographical expansion of the mission enterprise in the nineteenth century was as phenomenal as the multiplication of mission agencies. The rapidity of the development was not conducive to preliminary study of the theology of mission. There was a need for the Word of God in the world, and men and women responded willingly to the need. As they faced their opportunities and struggled with their problems the missionaries and mission agencies developed their policies and strategy. They did well. It is in the crucible of actual work that lasting principles can best be established.

On the other hand, it is difficult to arrive at a pure concept of mission if the formulation of the concept is partially predetermined by factors that impinge on the freedom of mission practice. Missions are conducted within history, and the missionary is a part of the period of history in which he works. Mission cannot remain theory and still be mission. It is dynamic action. It is action that takes place in the midst of humanity and must be geared to the humanity it serves. History will inevitably influence those who establish the policy and those who proclaim and hear the message of missions. Man is free to *think* a pure mission idea but not to practice it. The idea must be put to work within circumstances over which the missionary has no control.

The greatest qualifying factor of missions in the nineteenth century was colonialism. In earlier periods colonization had usually been among peoples of similar economic and cultural status. With the exception of the Hellenizing efforts of Alexander the Great no serious attempt to permanently change the cultural and economic patterns of peoples of the world had hitherto been made. Now colonialism, bringing Western culture with it, spread into Africa, parts of Asia, and into the islands of the South Pacific.

Whether the missionary was friendly or antagonistic to the colonizers, he was usually identified with them because of the color of his skin and because he arrived about the same time. If he came before the colonial power, which was most frequently the case, he was considered a "forerunner" of the occupation force. If he came later, or simultaneously, he was considered an agent of the conquerors.

There were incidents that gave some justification for the accusations. The Chinese, though never colonized, complained that missionaries gained access to their country by means of the treaty following the Opium War and that they depended on extraterritoriality to prosecute their work. The clause granting missionaries right of entering and preaching in China was not in the English version of the treaty but was in the agreement negotiated by France. Some French officials used the prestige of their position to support and protect French missionaries. Certainly other missionaries were guilty of using foreign prestige in their approach to the people, but it must be remembered that they constituted an insignificant minority. The incidents that justifiably rankled in the minds of the Chinese people were few compared to the multitudinous efforts of missionaries to help the people in every aspect of their lives in the true humility of the bearers of the Gospel. The many were branded by the action of the few. The missionaries could not change the color of their skin nor disavow their cultural heritage. Most of them regretted that the country was partially opened to them by political action and refused to use extraterritorial rights, which they found to be a handicap rather than a help.

Commendable as it may be for a missionary in China to condemn the gunboat policies of his government, or for another in India to identify himself with the nationalism in India rather than with his own fellow-countrymen, nevertheless there enter into the situation certain psychological and sociological connections with his own kith and kin which such personal repudiations cannot entirely sever. They constitute his social ancestry, which to a large extent have made him what he is. A man may be ashamed of his pedigree, or he may be proud of it; but nothing can alter the fact that the missionary is a man with a social and cultural genealogy, and this persists as a silent but inescapable element in the total impression which he makes upon other people. In like manner, the missionary is caught up in contemporaneous associations with the merchant, the tourist and the political representative; and these associations form an integral part of the total impression. Insofar as these have been reprehensible the missionary will do well to condemn; but denunciation alone is not sufficient to free him from his share of corporate responsibility. He is expected to do his utmost to rectify matters. As well might a man seek to separate himself from his shadow, as for a missionary to hope to emancipate himself entirely whether from the shadow of odium or the halo of glory which always accompany these corporate relationships.[1]

In the colonial expansion in Africa and in the South Pacific there were many different situations and varied reactions. No two nations had the same colonial policies, and the reactions of the people being colonized were partially dependent on the attitude of the colonizer. There were times when the native populace was grateful for colonization by a country that could establish law and order and would prevent colonization by another country with a less favorable policy.

No blanket judgment can be made on the results of colonization and its final influence on missions. The missionary proclaimed the Gospel, reduced the languages to writing, educated the people, established systems of medical care, and did what could be done for the people to elevate their status within the colonial setting. The colonial government supported evangelization in a few instances, but frequently was hostile to the total mission program. Popular education was frowned upon by some governments, strictly regulated by others. When the state religion of the colonizers was favored the work of the majority of missions was hampered and the favored church came to be recognized as an adjunct to political power. The missionary usually worked under a handicap in colonial territories. As rising nationalism became a factor in the twentieth century a very awkward situation arose. It was largely through the general enlightenment and special training of the people by the missions that the foundation for aspirations of independence was laid. The sympathy of the missionary lay with the people among whom he worked, and he was suspected by the government of collaboration with them in freedom movements. He was, at the same time, not quite trusted by most of the people. The missionary walked a tightrope in precarious balance between the two powers, trying to encourage the honest aspirations of the people at the same time that he attempted to live up to the regulations under which he had been accepted into the country as a guest of the government. In general, the missionary was ready to accept colonization "insofar as he was convinced that its presence was of benefit to the African himself. He was equally prepared to fight it, if it seemed to him that the rights of the African were being infringed or betrayed."[2] As the day for liberation of the colonies drew near, political activity by the missionary would have made the transition more difficult. His main task was to prepare the people and the churches for the coming day of freedom. Some of the difficulties experienced by missionaries and by Christians of the younger churches during this period are described by Dr. Neill.

> For both Indian Christians and missionaries, the years which preceded independence were a rather dreary time. Indian Christians were constantly accused by their fellow-countrymen of being "running-dogs of imperialism." This rankled in the minds of many, but especially of those who had wholeheartedly adopted the line of the Congress Party. These tended to take out their own inner unhappiness on their missionary friends by informing them that they were, perhaps unconsciously, agents of imperialism, that their motive in coming to India was not really the preaching of the Gospel but the propagation of western culture and European power. To such allegations no answer is possible. No human motives are entirely pure; no missionary could be absolutely certain that he had entirely freed himself from the contagions of race prejudice and western arrogance. The only thing to do was to suffer in silence, and to safeguard, as far as possible, friendly human relationship between Christians and non-Christians of diverse origins.[3]

Several lessons had been learned through the colonial period of the nineteenth century and the dissolution of colonies of the twentieth century that helped to serve as guide in establishing new mission policies. (1) The Christian mission must not be identified with a political power, nor become known as an agent of such power. (2) The message of mission must be geared to the understanding, the needs, and the sympathies of the people. (3) An indigenous church must be established as early as possible. This had been the aim through the nineteenth century, but with varied results. In a few instances the missionary staff had been withdrawn so early that the church they had left was undertrained so that it foundered and disintegrated. More often the transfer of responsibility was slowed down by an overcautious attitude of the founders of the mission. The psychology of the age, rather than the demands of the churches involved, hastened indigenization. At the time the colonies won their political freedom most of the churches had already had some years of experience taking responsibility under the leadership of their own pastors and officers.

Post-colonial problems are not all settled. No single set of policies will solve them. Each area and situation calls for specific solutions to be worked out with patience and understanding. Solutions are possible if the problems are faced and dealt with in the spirit of Christ.

Perhaps the most difficult problem of our generation is the question of the relationship of the Christian mission to non-Christian religions. This is not a new problem, but it has become more pressing in the past few decades. There are several reasons for this. The phenomenal development of education, industry, and technology in formerly underdeveloped nations has raised doubts in the minds of the people as to the compatibility of their own religions. The equality of men of recently liberated countries with men of former colonial powers in foreign relations and in international enclaves leads to self-examination and critical evaluation of other countries. Religions have not been exempt from this type of examination and comparison. The West has added to the problem as members of the school of humanism deal with religions on a sociological rather than a theological basis, speaking of cultural values rather than revealed truth. Questions as to the uniqueness of Christianity have been raised by critical schools of theology which have dissected the contents of the Christian message and have classified some of it with the myths of primitive religions. This is an age of restlessness, of change, of seeking new foundations and testing the old. It has led to the question of relationships sometimes spoken of as the confrontation of religions, the dialog of Christianity with other religions, or the conversation between religions.

Broad comparisons have been made between the religions of the

East and the religions of the West. Usually the West has been characterized as practical, the East as speculative and mystical. This is too broad a basis for conversations. Much of the mystical aspect of religions of the East comes from philosophical tendencies that may have only a very tenuous relationship to the religion, and much of the active nature of the religions of the West come from a deep spirituality. There are elements of Eastern religions that may seem shockingly concrete to the man of the West, and some obtuse speculative proposals of the West that may mystify the man of the East. Religions of world areas cannot be lumped together. Each has its own entity and character.

It has been implied by some that there is nothing unique in any religion so that union will be accomplished by simply admitting to a common goal. China has been pointed out as an example. Representatives from Confucianism, Taoism, and Buddhism may meet and officiate at the same wedding or funeral or be called in to a home at the time of family crises. This does not signify a blending of the three religions, however, nor even a conversation. Because a residual, pervading animism still dominates the religious life of the masses, some people want to assure themselves that no gods or spirits be offended by neglect. Such neglect may cause reprisals, while including all might bring good fortune. Taoism and Confucianism were originally political reform movements that became religions long after the deaths of the founders, by decree of the emperor and by the accretion of gods from early Chinese mythology.

The external aspects of religions—things which can be seen—become the basis for most comparison and conversation between religions. Among these we have ethics, worship, service, love, self-denial, other-worldliness and adherence to the teachings of the religion. By determining the superiority of these aspects it is thought that a true evaluation of the religions as a whole may be reached. Values within a religion will normally be reflected in the lives of its adherents, but become an unreliable standard of evaluation. As each religion has its own character, so it is a totality in itself. Every *aspect* of a religion assumes its character from the essential nature of the religion of which it is an external manifestation. Are its ethics a fruit of love in response to and as a result of God's act on behalf of man, or an attempt by man to manipulate God into granting him paradise or some physical blessing? Are meditation and adoration a natural thanksgiving for God's mercy or a means by which man can gain favor with the gods? What is the real character that lies behind the external visible aspects of a religion?

In the name of "conversation" between religions there has been an increasing tendency to find "Christian-like" aspects in other religions. This leads to comparisons wherein the Christian student is apt to ascribe Christian theological meanings to certain terms used in non-Christian religions that create a false concept of similarity. One instance is the claim, that is made with increasing insistence in our day by some students from the West, that Mahayana Buddhism is based on faith. When we speak of "faith" in reference to Christianity we speak of something that is not merely a teaching, but an act of God on man's behalf through which his sins are not overlooked but forgiven. God has acted and continues to act to redeem man, to give him a new birth, and to put a new spirit within him. It is faith *in God*, not faith *that* if *I do* certain things I will gain my desire. There is a difference between Christian faith and the faith of the adherent of the Pure Land Sect of Buddhism in China who believes that if he utters *Omitofu* at the time of death he will, as if by magic, be transported to the Western Paradise where he will eventually be given another opportunity to work out his own freedom from Samsara (the chain of transmigration).

> Just where the affinity is greatest, divergence reveals itself. A few instances of this will suffice. I have adverted to the "Lutheranism" of the Jodo and Shinshu sects in Japan. They preach salvation by faith, but not as the one possibility for sinning man; it is the "easy way" that is opened in this degenerate age. They proclaim a Savior and his grace, but they acknowledge that he never actually lived; he is a symbol and myth.[4]

Christianity is a faith—it is a *life* in faith. It is not a religion in the commonly accepted understanding of that term: Man's search for the eternal or his expression of faith in the eternal he has found. In the areas of *man's* search and expression, some comparison is possible. It is in this area where man speaks of superiority and inferiority. Insofar as a comparison is based on acts resulting from religious conviction some type of value judgment may be reached. However, such judgment is of the fringe aspects of faith, mixed with the human element of strength or weakness of the disciples, so its value is only relative.

> It would seem, therefore, that we cannot claim that Christianity is superior, if by this is meant some objective judgment on the religions. This does not mean that it is inferior, but simply that the language of superiority and inferiority is out of place in the sphere of religion, especially for the Christian. The religious spirit knows nothing of any compromise between itself and others, but only of the humility that comes from measuring itself by the divine holiness. From the standpoint of faith, comparison is out of the question. He to whom worship is offered is not superior to others, he is incomparable. The moment we begin to compare, we exchange the standpoint of the believer for that of the observer. Even there . . . the question of superiority is decided in advance by the standard employed for the comparison.[5]

We Christians frequently speak of faith as our response to the eternal God as he reaches out to us in grace. It is he that causes man to respond to the message of salvation which is the expression of his love. This message of God does not yield to human standards of comparison. It is God's confrontation with man. Mission is relating this message to all men. It is not the superior person offering something to an inferior. It is the sinner speaking to other sinners of the salvation that he has found in Christ.

There is value in a real or hypothetical meeting of religions of the world for conversation in clearing up false impressions of each other, to establish a climate of mutual understanding and respect, and to examine the possibility of united action in areas of human need and suffering. We must, however, realize the difficulty and limitations of such confrontations when they go beyond the area of the external and peripheral aspects of religion. Dr. Paul Tillich has made the rather paradoxical statement,

> that the main characteristic of the present encounter of the world religions is their encounter with the quasi-religions of our time. Even the mutual relations of the religions proper are decisively influenced by the encounter of each of them with secularism, and one or more of the quasi-religions which are based upon secularism.[6]

It may be added that it is in the quasi-religious area of each religion that most contacts between religions are being made. These do not actually portray or influence the religions participating in the discussion. In dealing with the essential nature and objective of each religion, there is a question whether the council table is the place where the final solution is to be reached. What can be accomplished by "religions" meeting "religions"?

Christ and the apostles did not sit as representatives of the Christian religion with the leaders of the religions of Rome and Greece. As the prophetic voice of Old Testament times, they spoke a message that penetrated through veneers of culture, self-glorification, and religion to reach the hearts of men. They condemned idolatry and all that was false. They attacked immoral and unethical practices among all peoples of all religions, not sparing the people of Israel nor members of the Christian church. Christianity, when true to its nature, is a disturbing factor in the world. It is disturbing because it calls all mankind to stand under the judgment of God. It is admittedly incomparable and incapable of yielding to syncretism. It is so, not only because it calls to judgment, but because it calls to salvation. It is this message that spontaneously creates true confrontation—in the hearts of men. It is God who confronts and man who makes response. It is not at the council-hall of religions where the real dialog takes place, but where man meets God, stripped of his religion, revealed as a sinner, and where God meets man as a Savior. To make this confrontation possible for all men is mission.

CHAPTER SIXTEEN

THE NEW DAY OF MISSION

Today one reads a great deal about the "new day of missions" due to changed conditions in the world and changed relationships between the West and other nations. There have been many so-called "new days" in the history of missions. Conditions have changed before, and adjustments in the attitudes and approach of missionaries and mission organizations have been necessary. Authority and responsibility have been shifted to the mission churches in order to preserve good Christian relationship and make possible continued effective work. Seldom in history, however, have changes been so rapid and far-reaching, so penetrating in their intensity and permanent in their results, as in the present day.

During World War II some mission societies of Europe found it impossible to give financial support and supply personnel. The churches on the mission fields responded with courage, showing spiritual maturity in assuming responsibility for the work, and in some instances giving financial help to missionaries who received no funds from the supporting agency. The situation hastened self-support and self-government. After the war, most missionaries who had been forced to leave returned to their fields of labor recognizing the new spirit of independence and the proven ability of the younger church to take responsibility.

In Indonesia the missionary was not welcomed back after the war. The indigenous churches there affiliated with international church organizations which gave the assistance needed to maintain the independence of the churches and the personnel needed to fill specific needs. The churches in Tanganyika were considered "orphaned" because the mission societies in Germany, due to political barriers, could not resume their support. There the various Lutheran churches received support from the Lutheran World Federation and were organized into a national federation of Lutheran churches with plans for one united Lutheran church in Tanganyika. A similar situation developed in New Guinea, but through more direct relationship with a mission board in America the German support continued—all support pooled for unified work in the mission.

Psychologically the World War had changed the relationships of the Western representative (in whatever capacity he had served) with the people of Africa, the Orient, and Southeast Asia. The peoples of these areas had fought side by side with the Westerner and against the Westerner. The men from East and West—the proud and the humble—had proven equally vulnerable to enemy fire. There were other leveling factors. Cultural differences were shrinking due to rapidly accelerated education in underdeveloped countries and new thirst for knowledge.

> The epoch is conditioned by a number of different factors. Intellectual and political changes have taken place in the non-Christian world, the field within which the Christian missionary activity has been carried on. They have come about to an extent, and with a rapacity, for which there is hardly a precedent in the history of earlier times. In the five years after the end of the war, not less than 1,250 million human beings, that is more than half the human race, have acquired a new political status. Changes in the political situation have been accompanied by changes in the structure of men's religious and intellectual conviction, and of their attitude to life and to the world. Missions are face to face with a considerable variety of situations; in some regions they have to do with ancient religions, which, with the political emancipation of their peoples have sprung into new life; elsewhere the old religions have been replaced by new quasi-religions of a political character. World-wide Communism has brought the Christian missions up against problems which have a special gravity of their own.[1]

Communist conquest of China closed that great land to mission activity. Other countries had previously been closed, but China, because of its size, its great population, and the extent to which missions had been conducted there, was of special significance. The final outcome cannot be determined, but for the time being, the churches there are standing the test of this difficult time without the direct support of mission agencies. As China was conquered by Communist force of arms, other nations of the Orient, South Seas, and Africa have faced a constant barrage of propaganda from the Communist press. This propaganda is insidious, given in the name of "freedom from the tyranny of Western imperialism" and "friendship for the underdeveloped peoples." Ruthless tactics and heavy pressure with ample financial support have helped to make an impact that missions have had to reckon with.

Developments within non-Christian religions have also had effect on the mission program. Islam has become more militant. England and France had long catered to Islam during colonial days and in certain areas entered into agreements that seriously hampered mission advance. Now several countries are under complete domination of a Muslim majority. Iraq and Sudan have been added to the number of Islamic countries where Christian missions are excluded. It is possible that other countries will adopt similar regulations. Simultaneously an aggressive Muslim spirit is manifested in areas of Tanzania and in sections of Nigeria and Cameroun where special concessions and favored treatment are demanded from the government.

Less serious is the resurgence of pagan religions. A great deal of significance was seen in the reawakening of Buddhist, Hindu, and primitive religions, in certain areas, closely associated with the new nationalism that was born with the demise of colonialism. Actually, the reawakening of an old religion on that basis will not last as long as the emotional nationalism that caused it. It can cause temporary disturbances and frustrations, but when the extraneous reason for its resurgence subsides, the message of the Gospel will again reach people of these faiths as it has in the past.

In establishing mission policy for our day, it is necessary to take into consideration the spirit of freedom among the nations. Freedom has come as a long-desired reality to many. It is still the burning desire and hope for others. Some who found freedom from colonialism have learned that freedom is a blessing which requires constant diligence, not something that is won once for all. Some who have won freedom from foreign rule have come under a new bondage more severe than colonialism. The concern for freedom belongs to the mission concept. It was first engendered in the hearts of the people of Asia and Africa by the Gospel message, and was nurtured by the mission schools. From earliest mission history there was the hope that indigenous churches might take over the responsibility for the evangelization of their own people and for the government and maintenance of their church. Though that was the goal, the process had often fallen into patterns that were scheduled at a slower pace than new developments called for.

There were special cases causing difficulties for missions. India demanded that missionaries should not be admitted to the country unless they could prove that they had the needed skills that could not be provided by the Indian Christians. Basically such a decision was reasonable, but the needs of a church could not be easily categorized. The degree of nationalistic spirit, the ambitions or jealousies among Christians or non-Christians might often play a part in the interpretation of the government position. Indonesia's stand against any foreign assistants in the church was modified when it became apparent that special situations and tasks demanded help from abroad. The position of such a worker in the life of the church brought problems. In other lands too, special cases developed where loving patience, rather than a radically new policy, was needed in order that the work could progress in a spirit of unity.

The signs of the times were misread by many. The slogan "Missionary Go Home" was taken seriously by some. Cyrus L. Sulzberger of the *New York Times* in a column datelined Uganda, 1965, used the headline, "As the Missionary's Era Ends." Reaction to this impression, on the part of some missions, was like entering a race to see who could "be the first to go the farthest" in disenfranchising the missionary, even before the churches abroad were ready to take over all the burdens that had been carried by the missionaries. The confusion of this period, frequently precipitated by mission boards taking hasty action without judicious deliberation with those concerned, left some missionaries feeling suddenly useless as their assignments were cancelled and their responsibilities transferred to others. What actually happened was the unconscious repudiation of the missionary calling. Mistakes could have been avoided if the validity of mission as a necessary integral part of the church had been constantly kept in mind. Then the missionaries of the West and of Africa and the East would have continued as brothers in working out a solution—the question of "mission" versus "church" would have dissolved in their common zeal for the evangelization of the world.

In South Africa, where freedom has not yet been granted to the dark-skinned by the white government, the Lutheran Church (a joint organization of churches from six separate missions from America, Norway, Sweden, and Germany) has been given responsibility for conducting church affairs. Missionaries are assigned their special tasks and places of residence by the church. Policies and activities within rural and urban areas are the responsibility of the church. There is no antagonism against the "European" (white) missionaries, but requests are made that they remain and that additional workers be sent.

In Northern Nigeria the pagan tribes were traditionally ruled by Moslems as a result of previous conquest. Where free elections were held after liberation from colonial rule, the pagans elected their own chiefs. One of those elected, who was also elected to serve in the national assembly, was a Christian, a member of the church council, and chairman of its evangelism program. Five hundred laymen were in the program. Each one would sell his land or business and move to an unevangelized area. There, as a layman, he established a new home or business, and witnessed of Christ till congregations were formed and a Bible school trainee or theological graduate could be called and stationed there. Then he would move on to a new area where there was no Christian witness. This response to the new responsibility for evangelism was heartening.

It has been discovered that the day of missions is not over. Some elements in our concepts of the mission of the church are unchanged, but many of the basic concepts are found in new relationships and new emphases. The new age has confronted the church anew with the concept of mission in its elemental evangelical forms and has sought new means of communication in the modern world.

1. Mission is considered objectively as inherent in the nature of the church. Mission is not the response to a special need, but is the life-breath of the church at all times.

> Hartenstein interprets the findings of Willingen in the following terms: "The being of the Church consists in its participation in God's plan of salvation, in His mission for the redemption of the world. The missionary enterprise reveals the deepest meaning of the Church as that Body which is sent by God, as

the new humanity, as the firstfruits of redemption. It is impossible to speak rightly of the Church, without speaking of its mission to the world. The Church exists in its missionary activity."[2]

Despite the confusion about the meaning of "mission" in both the East and West, where some persons erroneously identify it with a sending operation of Western churches, there is emerging with increasing clarity the understanding that mission is the primary function of the Church between the Ascension and the full coming of God's Kingdom. What mission is can most simply be stated in the Biblical affirmation that "God was in Christ reconciling the world unto Himself," and that God has committed to the Church this ministry of reconciliation.[3]

2. The realization that mission is a vital part of the church, from which it cannot be separated—and still remain the church—lays the burden of mission equally on all churches of every nation in every stage of development.

Both older and younger churches need to understand missions as activities within the world mission of the church. Within that world mission there is room for inter-church aid. A church which feels that its own responsibility has been discharged when the new church is established as a self-governing, and wholly or largely self-supporting body, has never rightly understood its missionary responsibility. "If you want to go home when we have achieved a responsible existence of our own, you should never have come," said the Asian Christian leader, Dr. D. T. Niles not long ago.[4]

3. The church is universal and world-wide. There is no East and West in the church under Christ. There is a new bond of understanding and fellowship between the older churches that have sent missionaries and the younger churches that have received their testimony.

There is a steadily growing conviction among Christians, partly as a result of the deeper understanding of the Bible, and partly as a result of the ecumenical movement, that this word "autonomy" cannot be used of the individual believer of his Church without qualifications.[5]

The Church can live only if the branch is attached to the vine. Hence, there can be no purely independent existence of the

Church not even in its capacity as His Body. This has nothing to do with the humanist idea of self-realization. . . . Thus the truly responsible nature of the Church and the development towards it are nothing but an expression in the life of the Church of the relation between justification and sanctification. A theology of Mission which sees the declaration of responsibility as the end of a process of development is guilty of teaching "justification by works." The one foundation of the Church is Christ's unique act of redemption which we must try again and again to comprehend through faith.[6]

Being of the same body, there is no essential difference, either in position or responsibility, between the older and younger churches before God. Together they are *the church* through which God speaks in the world. There are matters which may require adjustments in the new period of freedom, but the magnitude of the task of evangelism demands all available personnel, and personal differences must disappear in the work that is shared by Christians of every race and nation. Where a working partnership has been established between missionary and national worker, in Christ, difficulties are no greater than those which normally occur in any large organization where members of the staff may have different backgrounds.

4. The magnitude of the problems that face the church today, and the realization that the church is dependent on its spiritual resources alone to meet and solve them, has created a change in the general picture of missions. For many years Christian missions pioneered in the struggle to bring the blessings of the Gospel, literacy, adequate medical care and freedom to oppressed people of the world. Help in the work was at times given by governments where missionaries served, by other humanitarian groups, or by the supporting church in the West. Missions were given special prestige and won adherents because of the humanitarian services rendered, in addition to the respect and love they won from converts because of their purely spiritual ministry. Missions had a certain advantage through humanitarian services that added to the success of its total program.

At present it is, in principle, short of this "advantage." If one may use this word with great critical reservations. I myself count this one of the unintended blessings of secularization, including the fact that the Church in many of its historical dominions is more and more decreasing into a minority. If the

Church sees this and seizes it in the realism of faith, that is to say, with a robust trust in the power of the Holy Spirit, it will discover the sustaining power of continuity and prestige as being merely crutches, and will be glad to strive forth in faith, in the power of the forces inherent in its nature and calling.[7]

Today other agencies are also active in medicine and literacy—in some areas, exclusively due to government regulations. In one sense this is a relief for the church. As long as such services were necessary, the church willingly performed them in the name of Christ. Where the government has taken them over, the force of the mission can be concentrated in the area of evangelism which is the root from which other services will grow from within the indigenous church. The church in our day must rely not on prestige resulting from social services rendered, but on the power of the Holy Spirit given at Pentecost. This may result in a whole new era of advance of the church.

5. There has come to the newer churches, in what were formerly called "mission lands," a new appreciation of the historical church. The churches in the new nations have awakened to a better understanding of the place of the church in history as something broader than the practice of individuals and organizations. They have sensed the unity of faith, purpose, and strength that come from the continuation of history, flowing in the same spirit, through the church of the present.

This unity is not only in a historical organization but in the church as God's creation for the purpose of bringing the Gospel to all the world. Recently organized churches have joined hands with those that brought the message to them, in mission extension to others. The result is a spontaneous witness to the people of the local areas and tribes, and through organized mission work abroad.

As a new tide is running in the evangelistic outreach of the younger churches, so their missionary outreach is beginning to gather momentum. More and more they are sending out their own missionaries, organizing their missionary agencies, and putting before their people the opportunity to participate in the world-wide witness of the Christian mission. This movement is spreading so rapidly that any list one could make of missionaries sent out by these churches would be out of date before it could be printed. Missionaries from churches in India are serving in Sumatra, Malaya, Nepal, and other places. Batak

Christians from Sumatra are serving as missionaries in Sarawak and other islands. The Church of Viet-Nam has nine "foreign" missionary couples. Cambodia is represented by a missionary in Thailand. The Karen Christians of Burma have sent their sons to minister to the Karens within Thailand. Japanese Christians are serving in South America as well as in other Asian countries. The United Church of Christ in the Philippines has missionaries serving in Indonesia and Thailand.[8]

This list of missions and missionaries could be enlarged. Most countries where missions are conducted are asking for more missionaries.

The day of Missions is not over till the day of the church is over. The church's vitality is in its mission, to which it is called and driven by the Holy Spirit. This mission does not decrease because of difficulties or problems. There are different situations to be faced in each generation. Mission is increased by the addition of each new church in each new area of the world. Mission will continue till the consummation of our age in the return of the risen Lord.

FOOTNOTES

INTRODUCTION

1. Hendrik Kraemer, *The Christian Message in a Non-Christian World* (New York: Harper and Brothers, 1938), p. 30.

CHAPTER ONE

1. Cf. M. Carus-Wilson, *The Expansion of Christendom* (London: Hodder and Stoughton, 1931), pp. 7-37.
2. Cotton Mather, *A Discourse Delivered for the Propagation of the Gospel Among the American Indians* (Boston: B. Green, 1721), pp. 62-70.
3. Carus-Wilson, *op. cit.*, p. 22.
4. Joseph Tracy, *History of American Missions to the Heathen from Their Commencement to the Present Time* (Worcester: Spooner and Howland, 1840).
5. Carus-Wilson, *op. cit.*, p. 19.
6. Hendrik Kraemer, *Religion and the Christian Faith* (Philadelphia: The Westminster Press, 1956), p. 30.
7. J. H. Bavinck, *An Introduction to the Science of Missions* (Philadelphia: Presbyterian and Reformed Publishing Co., 1960), p. xix.

8. Nicolas Berdyaev, *The Destiny of Man*, New York: Scribner and Sons, 1937), p. 165.
9. Emil Brunner, *The Word and the World* (London: S.C.M. Press, 1931), p. 108. Published and distributed in the U.S. by Charles Scribner and Sons.
10. Gerald H. Anderson, *The Theology of the Christian Mission* (New York: McGraw-Hill Book Co., 1961), p. 79. Used by permission of McGraw-Hill Book Co.
11. Edwin A. Lewis, *A Philosophy of the Christian Revelation* (New York: Harper and Brothers, 1940), pp. 75-76.
12. Andrew L. Drummond, *German Protestantism Since Luther* (London: The Epworth Press, 1951), p. 62.
13. Lesslie Newbigin, *Trinitarian Faith and Today's Mission* (Richmond: John Knox Press, 1964), p. 30.

CHAPTER TWO

1. *Lutheran Hymnary* (Minneapolis: Augsburg Publishing House, 1913), No. 132.
2. Robert Hall Glover, *The Bible Emphasis of Missions* (Chicago:

Moody Press, 1964), p. 14. Used by permission of Moody Press, Moody Bible Institute of Chicago.

3. Gerhard von Rad, "Typological Interpretation of the Old Testament," in Claus Westermann, *Essays on Old Testament Interpretation* (London: S.C.M. Press, 1963), p. 27.

4. Hans G. Conzelmann, "The First Christian Century, As Christian History," in J. Philip Hyatt, *The Bible in Modern Scholarship* (Nashville: Abingdon Press, 1965), p. 220.

5. Johannes Blauw, *The Missionary Nature of the Church* (New York: McGraw-Hill, 1962), pp. 17, 18. Used by permission of McGraw-Hill Book Co.

6. Bengt Sundkler, *Missionens Värld* (Stockholm Diakonistyrelsens Bokförlag, 1963), p. 2 (In translation). Published by Aktiebolaget Svenska Bokforlaget.

7. Gerhard von Rad, *Old Testament Theology* (Edinburgh: Oliver and Boyd, 1962), Vol. 1, p. 140.

8. Blauw, *op. cit.*, p. 18.

9. Max Warren, *The Christian Imperative* (New York: Charles Scribner and Sons, 1955), p. 24.

10. Rad, *op. cit.*, p. 149.

11. Blauw, *op. cit.*, p. 19.

12. Ernest G. Wright, "The Old Testament Basis for the Christian Missions" in G. Anderson, *The Theology of the Christian Mission* (New York: McGraw-Hill Book Co., 1961), p. 23. Used by permission of McGraw-Hill Book Co.

13. Cf. Num. 22:1-18; Joshua 2:1-21; 2 Kings 5:1-14; Ex. 18:1-12.

14. Cf. Ex. 22:22; 23:1-9.

15. Martin Buber, *Israel and Palestine* (London: East and West Library, 1952), pp. x-xi.

16. Max Warren, *The Christian Mission* (London: S.C.M. Press, 1951), p. 12. Published in the U.S. by Friendship Press.

17. Blauw, *op. cit.*, p. 47.

18. Cf. Ps. 2, 18, 20, 21, 45, 72, 89, 101, 110, 132.

19. Cf. Jer. 30:9; 33:14-16; Ezek. 34: 22-30; 37:24-28; Hag. 2:7-9; Zech. 6:9-15; Zeph. 3:9.

20. Karl Barth, *Church Dogmatics* (Edinburgh: T. & T. Clark, 1956), Vol. 4, Part 1, p. 28.

21. H. H. Rowley, *The Missionary Message of the Old Testament* (London: The Carey Press, 1946), p. 53.

CHAPTER THREE

1. Frederick Derwacter, *Preparing the Way for Paul* (New York: The Macmillan Co., 1930), pp. 68-69.

2. Derwacter, *op. cit.*, p. 119.

3. Ferdinand Hahn, *Mission in the New Testament* (Chatham: S.C.M. Press, 1965), p. 22. Distributed in the U.S. by Alec R. Allenson Inc., Naperville, Ill.

4. Derwacter, *op. cit.*, pp. 86-87.

CHAPTER FOUR

1. Blauw, *op. cit.*, p. 66.

2. Hendrik Kraemer, *The Christian Message in a Non-Christian World* (New York: Harper and Brothers, 1938, p. 70.

3. Max Warren, *The Christian Imperative*, p. 22.

4. Cf. Luke 1:32-33; 1:46-55; 2: 29-33.

5. Hahn, *op. cit.*, pp. 29-30.

6. Cf. Matt. 23:1-36.

7. Cf. Matt. 11:16-24; Luke 4:24-27.

8. Adolph Harnack, *The Mission and Expansion of the Church*

(New York: Harper Torchbook, 1961), cf. pp. 36-43.

9. Cf. Mark 7:24-37; Luke 4:42—5:1; 5:17; John 4:1-42; Luke 9:51-56.

10. Cf. Luke 7:1-10; John 4:46-54.

11. Cf. Luke 9:1-5; Mark 6:7-11; Luke 10:1-12.

12. Hahn, *op. cit.*, p. 45.

13. Anderson, *op. cit.*, p. 46.

14. Cf. Mark 16:14-18; Luke 24:44-52; John 20:19-23; Acts 1:6-11; Matt. 9:37.

15. Blauw, *op. cit.*, p. 83.

16. Anderson, *op. cit.*, pp. 55-56.

CHAPTER FIVE

1. Adolf Harnack, *op. cit.*, pp. 19-22.

2. Cf. Acts 8:4-40.

3. Johannes Munck, *Paul and the Salvation of Mankind* (Richmond, Va.: John Knox Press, 1959), p. 71.

4. Munck, *op. cit.*, p. 26.

5. Cf. Luke 17:23-37; 21:5-28; 2 Thess. 2:1-12.

6. Cf. Acts 7:58—8:1; 9:1-22; 22:1-16; Gal. 1:13-15; Phil. 3:4-7.

7. Cf. Eph. 4:3-6; Rom. 12:4; 1 Cor. 12:12-27.

8. Martin Schlunk, *Paulus als Missionar* (Gütersloh: Verlag C. Bertelsmann, 1937), p. 96 (Translation).

9. Cf. 1 Tim. 3:1-13; 5:1-22.

CHAPTER SIX

1. Lemuel C. Barnes, *Two Thousand Years of Missions before Carey* (Chicago: The Christian Culture Press, American Baptist Society, 1900), p. 42.

2. *The Interpreter's Dictionary of the Bible* (Nashville: Abingdon Press, 1962), Vol. 2, p. 118.

3. Barnes, *op. cit.*, p. 70.

4. Alexander Roberts and James Donaldson, Ed., *The Ante-Nicene Fathers* (Buffalo, N.Y.: The Christian Literature Co., 1886), VIII 704-705.

5. Kenneth Scott Latourette, *A History of the Expansion of Christianity* (New York: Harper and Brothers, 1937), Vol. 1, p. 101.

6. W. A. Wigram, *An Introduction to the History of the Assyrian Church* (London: S.P.C.K.; New York: E. S. Gorham, 1910), p. 26

7. Latourette, *op. cit.*, Vol. 1, p. 103

8. Barnes, *op. cit.*, p. 89.

9. S. G. Pothan, *The Syrian Christians of Kerala* (London: Asia Publishing House, 1963), pp. 5-6.

10. Tertullian, "On Idolatry," from *Early Latin Theology*, tr. by S. L. Greenslade. *The Library of Christian Classics* (Philadelphia: The Westminster Press, 1956), Vol. 83. Used by permission.

11. From *Early Christian Fathers*, tr. by Cyril C. Richardson. *The Library of Christian Classics* (Philadelphia: The Westminster Press, 1953), Vol. I, p. 214. Used by permission.

12. *Ibid.*, p. 245.

13. Latourette, *op. cit.*, Vol. I, pp. 111-112.

CHAPTER SEVEN

1. F. Crawford Burkitt, *Early Christianity Outside the Roman Empire* (London: C. J. Clay and Sons, 1889), Cf. p. 38 ff.

2. Latourette, *op. cit.*, Vol. 1, p. 230.

3. Hendrik Kraemer, *The Communication of the Christian Faith* (Philadelphia: The Westminster Press, 1956), pp. 43-44. Copyright 1956, W. L. Jenkins. Used by permission.

4. G. D. Mallech, *History of the Syrian Nation and the Old Evangelical Church of the East* (Minneapolis: Augsburg Publishing House, 1954), p. 3.

5. Juhanon Mar Thomas, *Christianity in India and a Brief History of the Mar Thoma Syrian Church* (Madras, India: K. M. Cherian, 1954), p. 3.

6. *Ibid.*, p. 7.

7. Barnes, *op. cit.*, p. 91.

8. Thomas, *op. cit.*, pp. 13-14.

9. John Foster, *The Church of the T'ang Dynasty* (London: S.P.C.K., 1939), p. 8.

10. A. C. Moule, *Christians in China Before 1550* (London: S.P.C.K., 1930), pp. 38-41. (Selections.)

11. Foster, *op. cit.*, pp. 51-52.

12. Latourette, *op. cit.*, Vol. 2, p. 280.

CHAPTER EIGHT

1. Joseph Schmidlin, *Catholic Mission History* (Techny, Ill.; Mission Press S.V.D., 1933), p. 107. Reprinted with permission from Divine Word Publications, Techny, Ill.

2. Robert Hall Glover, *The Progress of World Wide Missions* (New York: Harper and Brothers, 1960), p. 24.

3. Schmidlin, *op. cit.*, p. 123.

4. Schmidlin, *op. cit.*, p. 165.

5. *Ibid.*, 175-176.

6. James Thayer Addison, *The Medieval Missionary* (New York: 1963), pp. 140-141. Courtesy of the Division of World Mission and Evangelism of the World Council of Churches.

7. Glover, *op. cit.*, p. 28.

8. Addison, *op. cit.*, p. 22.

9. *Ibid.*, pp. 37-38.

10. *Ibid.*, p. 45.

11. *Ibid.*, p. 49.

CHAPTER NINE

1. Gertrude Aulen, *Kristendomens väg til Folken* (Stockholm: Svenska Kyrkans diakonistyrelses bokforlag, 1939), p. 477 (Translation).

2. H. Ussing, *Evangeliets Seiersgang* (Denmark: Universitetsboghandler G.E.C. Gad, 1902), p. 29 (Translation).

3. Hendrik Kraemer, *The Communication of the Christian Faith* (Philadelphia: The Westminster Press, 1956), pp. 51-52.

4. Norman A. Horner, *Cross and Crucifix in Mission* (New York: Abingdon Press, 1965), p. 27.

5. A. C. Moule, *Christians in China Before 1550* (London: S.P.C.K., 1930), pp. 136-137.

6. Kenneth Scott Latourette, *A History of Christian Missions in China* (New York: Macmillan Co., 1929), p. 69.

7. Schmidlin, *op. cit.*, p. 330.

8. Theodore Maynard, *The Odyssey of Francis Xavier* (London: Longemans, Green & Co., 1936), p. 32. Used by permission of David McKay Company, Inc.

9. Maynard, *op. cit.*, pp. 118-119.

10. Julius Richter, *A History of Missions in India* (London: Oliphant Anderson & Ferrier, 1908), p. 49. Used by permission of Marshall, Morgan & Scott.

11. J. N. Ogilvie, *The Apostles of India* (London: Hodder & Stoughton, 1860), p. 187.

12. Otis Cary, *A History of Christianity in Japan* (New York: Fleming H. Revell Co., 1909), p.. 41.

13. Maynard, *op. cit.*, p. 283.

14. Katherin Carr Rodell, *South American Primer* (New York: Harcourt, Brace & World, Inc., 1941), p. 14.

15. Cf. George P. Howard, *Religious Liberty in Latin America?* (Philadelphia: Westminster Press, 1944), and Stanley W. Rycroft, *Religion and Faith in Latin America* (Philadelphia: Westminster Press, 1958).

CHAPTER TEN

1. John Nicholas Lenker, *Luther's Works* (Minneapolis: Lutherans in All Lands Company, 1907), Vol. 12, pp. 201-202.

2. Jaroslav Pelikan, Ed., *Luther's Works* (St. Louis: Concordia Publishing House, 1958), Vol. 14, p. 9.

3. Martin Luther, *The German Mass and Order of Service 1526* (Philadelphia: Muhlenberg Press), Vol. 6, pp. 172-173. By permission of Fortress Press.

4. Cf. Niels Aage Barfoed, *Hans Egede, Grönlands Apostel* (Stavanger, Norway: Missionsselskapets Forlag, 1950). General history of the mission.

5. Louis Bobe, *Hans Egede, Colonizer and Missionary of Greenland* (Copenhagen: Rosenkilde and Bagger, 1952), p. 162.

CHAPTER ELEVEN

1. Andrew L. Drummond, *German Protestantism Since Luther* (London: Epworth League, 1951), p. 53.

2. *Ibid.*, p. 60.

3. Ussing, *Evangeliets Seiersgang*, p. 87 (Translation).

4. A. Lehmann, *It Began at Tranquebar* (India: Christian Literature Society, 1956), p. 171.

CHAPTER TWELVE

1. A. J. Lewis, *Zinzendorf, the Ecumenical Pioneer* (S.C.M. Press Ltd., 1962. Published 1962 Westminster Press, U.S.A.), pp. 24-25. Used by permission.

2. *Ibid.*, pp. 79-80.

3. S. Baudert, "Zinzendorf's Thought on Missions Related to His Views of the World." I.R.M. 21:83 (July, 1932), p. 395.

4. J. E. Hutton, *A History of Moravian Missions* (London: Moravian Publication Office, 1922), p. 21.

5. *Ibid.*, pp. 44-45.

6. *Ibid.*, p. 103.

7. *Ibid.*, pp. 74.

CHAPTER THIRTEEN

1. Stephen Neill, *A History of Christian Missions* (Baltimore: Penguin Books, 1964), p. 261.

2. Wolfgang Eberhard Löwe, *The First American Foreign Missionaries.* A dissertation for partially satisfying the requirements of a Ph.D. degree at Brown University. (Ann Arbor, Mich.: University Microfilms, Inc., 1962), p. 38.

3. *Ibid.*, p. 76.

4. Kenneth Latourette, *The History of the Expansion of Christianity*, Vol. 4, pp 47-51.

CHAPTER FOURTEEN

1. Stephen Neill, *A History of Christian Missions* (Baltimore: Penguin Books, 1964), pp. 259-360.

2. Peter Beyerhaus and Henry Le-fever, *The Responsible Church and the Foreign Mission* (Grand Rapids: Eerdmans Publishing House, 1964), p. 33.

3. Herman Schlyter, *Karl Gutzlaff als Missionar in China* (Lund: C.W.K. Gleerup, 1964), p. 137 (Translation).

4. *Op cit.*, p. 158.

5. Latourette, *A History of Christian Missions in China* (New York: Macmillan Co., 1929), p. 254. Reprinted with permission of the Macmillan Co.

6. *World Missionary Conference, 1910*, Edinburgh (New York: Fleming & Revell Co., 1910), Vol. 9, pp. 347-350.

7. A. Lehman, *Mission zwischen Gestern und Morgen* (Stuttgart: Evang. Missionsverlag, 1952), p. 8.

8. Jerusalem Meeting of the International Missionary Conference 1928 (New York: I. M. C., 1928), Vol. 1, pp. 401-402.

9. Ernest Troeltsch, *Christian Thought, Its History and Application* (New York: George H. Doran Co., 1923).

10. William Hocking, *Living Religions and a World Faith* (New York: Macmillan Co., 1940), p. 22.

11. Homan, "I Don't Want to Christianize the World," *Christian Century* 52: 1483-4.

12. Oscar Macmillan Buck, *Christianity Tested* (New York: Abingdon Press, 1934), p. 146.

13. Albert Schweitzer, *Out of My Life and Thought* (New York: Bolton Company, 1933), p. 227.

14. Hendrik Kraemer, *The Christian Message in a Non-Christian World* (New York: Harper and Brothers), pp. 134-135.

15. Hendrik Kraemer, *Madras Series*, Vol. 1 (New York: International Missionary Council, 1939), p. 1.

16. Hartenstein, *Das Wunder der Kirche*, p. 194.

17. Wilhelm Andersen, *Towards a Theology of Mission* (London: S.C.M. Press Ltd., 1955), p. 21.

18. *Ibid.*, p. 10.

19. Max A. C. Warren, "The Thought and Practice of Mission" in *Basileia* edited by Jan Hermelink and Hans Jochen Margull (Stuttgart: Evang. Missionsverlag, 1961), pp. 162-163.

20. Andersen, *op. cit.*, p. 40.

21. *Ibid.*, p. 23.

22. *Ibid.*, p. 23.

CHAPTER FIFTEEN

1. Archibald G. Baker, *The Christian Missions and a New World Culture* (Chicago: Willet, Clark & Co., 1943), p. 48. Reprinted with the permission of Harper & Row, Publishers, Inc.

2. Stephen Neill, *Colonialism and Christian Missions* (New York: McGraw-Hill Book Company, 1966), p. 309.

3. *Ibid.*, p. 113.

4. E. L. Allen, *Christianity Among the Religions* (Boston: Beacon Press, 1960), p. 148.

5. *Ibid.*, pp. 131-132.

6. Paul Tillich, *Christianity and the Encounter of the World Religions* (New York: Columbia University Press, 1963), pp. 4-5.

CHAPTER SIXTEEN

1. Wilhelm Andersen, *Towards a Theology of Mission* (London: S.C.M. Press Ltd., 1956), p. 12. Quote is from W. Freytag, K. Hartenstein, and A. Lehmann, *Mission zwischen Gestern und*

Morgen, p. 4. Distributed in the U.S. by Friendship Press.

2. *Ibid.,* p. 54.

3. R. Pierce Beaver, *The Christian World Mission — A Reconsideration* (Calcutta, India, Baptist Mission Press, 1957), p. v. Used by permission of the Carey, Kingsgate Press Ltd.

4. Peter Beyerhaus and Henry Lefever, *The Responsible Church and the Foreign Mission,* p. 12.

Used by permission of Eerdman's Publishing Co.

5. *Ibid.,* p. 16.

6. *Ibid.,* p. 133.

7. Hendrik Kraemer, *The Communication of the Christian Faith* (Philadelphia: The Westminster Press, 1956), p. 115.

8. Eugene L. Smith, *God's Mission —And Ours* (New York: Abingdon Press, 1961), pp. 38-39.

266.009
Sy 9

Date Due